Managing Editor: Rick Joyner
Contributing Editors: Jack Deere, Francis Frangipane, Dudley Hall
Assistant Editor: Deborah Joyner Johnson
Layout and Design: Dana Zondory
Cover Design: Kevin Lepp
Copy Editors: Cheryl Anderson, Suzanne Hirt, Deborah Williams, and Sarah Williams

The Morning Star Journal® USPS012-903 is published quarterly, 4 issues per year, by MorningStar Publications, Inc., a division of MorningStar Fellowship Church, 375 Star Light Drive, Fort Mill, SC 29715. Fall 2007 issue. Periodicals postage rates paid at Wilkesboro, NC and additional mailing offices. CPC Agreement #1472593. ISSN# 10832122

POSTMASTER: Send address corrections to *The Morning Star Journal*®, 375 Star Light Drive, Fort Mill, SC 29715

Subscription rates: One year $20.00; Outside U.S. $30.00 USD.

MorningStar Publications is a non-profit organization dedicated to the promulgation of important teachings and timely prophetic messages to the church. We also attempt to promote interchange between the different streams and denominations in the body of Christ.

To receive a subscription to *The Morning Star Journal*®, send payment along with your name and address to *MorningStar Publications*, 375 Star Light Drive, Fort Mill, SC 29715, (803) 802-5544 (1-800-542-0278—Credit Card Orders Only); fax (704) 285-7251. One year (4 quarterly issues) U.S. $20.00; Outside U.S. $24.95 USD. Prices are subject to change without notice.

All Scripture references are from the New American Standard Bible unless otherwise specified. In this Journal, NAS refers to the New American Standard Bible, © 1960, 1962, 1963, 1968, 1971, 1973, 1974, 1977, by the Lockman Foundation. NKJV refers to the Holy Bible, New King James Version, © 1979, 1980, 1982 by Thomas Nelson, Inc. NIV refers to the Holy Bible: New International Version®, NIV®, © 1973, 1978, 1984 by International Bible Society. AMP refers to The Amplified Bible, © 1954, 1958, 1962, 1964, 1965 by Zondervan Publishing House. RSV refers to The Revised Standard Version, © 1962 by The Word Publishing Co. TLB refers to The Living Bible, © 1971 by Tyndale House Publishers. ASV refers to the American Standard Version. ESV refers to English Standard Version, © 2001 by Crossway Bibles a division of Good News Publishing. Italics in Scripture references are for emphasis only.

THE
MORNING STAR JOURNAL
VC
N

STRONG FOUNDATIONS

2 THE MYSTERY OF HISTORY
DUDLEY HALL

8 FREEDOM THROUGH FORGIVENESS
DEBORAH JOYNER JOHNSON

12 JUSTICE, LAW, AND LEGALISM—PART I
AN ORTHODOX JEWISH RABBI

THE OVERCOMING LIFE

23 THE STRONGHOLD OF CHRIST'S LIKENESS
FRANCIS FRANGIPANE

28 THE GOSPEL TRUTH
RICK JOYNER

38 SPIRIT-FILLED MINISTRY
LARRY KREIDER

42 THE LANGUAGE OF THE SPIRIT
RICK JOYNER

THE GREAT SOCIETY

53 DOMESTICATED CHRISTIANITY
LARRY OCASIO

PROPHETIC PERSPECTIVES

58 THE RELIGIOUS SPIRIT
BOB JONES AND PAUL KEITH DAVIS

66 THE HOLY SPIRIT AND THE ARTS
RICK JOYNER AND AMANDA PRYCHODKO

75 A CHRISTIAN APPROACH TO THE ENVIRONMENT
ANNA JANE JOYNER

STRONG FOUNDATIONS

Growing Stronger, Deeper Roots in Sound Biblical Truth

The Mystery of History

by Dudley Hall

Everyone likes a mystery—even God. He actually wrote one. It is commonly called *history.* In a good mystery you often know the ending but you don't know the twists that get you there. Once you know the ending, you start looking back over the story to find all the clues you saw and the ones you did not see. The more you go back over it, the more you see what was missed the first time. God devised history in a way that those with submissive hearts would see things which proud hearts would always miss.

Full understanding for anyone, however, requires an explanation from the author. If we are to understand the mystery as explained in the New Testament, there are several essential passages of Scripture that I recommend you read carefully: Ephesians 3:1-13; Colossians 1:24-29; and Romans 11:25-28, 16:25. Each of these passages express common aspects, but also add a bit more to understanding the mystery that can only be explained in Jesus, the Messiah.

One of the most obvious aspects was the persecution that Paul endured because he understood the mystery while many of his contemporaries did not. It seems that when others don't see the keys to the story, they get very angry at those who do. Paul was continually accused of being against the Jews, the temple, and the Law. This reveals to us that their understanding of history did not encompass what God had revealed to Paul through the risen Christ, and without that vital piece of evidence, history comes to a wrong conclusion.

Now I rejoice in my sufferings for your sake, and in my flesh I am filling up what is lacking in Christ's afflictions for the sake of his body, that is, the church,

of which I became a minister according to the stewardship from God that was given to me for you, to make the word of God fully known,

the mystery hidden for ages and generations but now revealed to his saints.

To them God chose to make known how great among the Gentiles are the riches of the glory of this mystery, which is Christ in you, the hope of glory.

Him we proclaim, warning everyone and teaching everyone with all wisdom, that we may present everyone mature in Christ.

For this I toil, struggling with all his energy that he powerfully works within me (Colossians 1:24-29 ESV).

The story of history moves from partial to full, shadow to substance, and natural to spiritual.

So How Do We Interpret History?

First, we must recognize that history is not self-evident. That is, we cannot find the meaning by just knowing all the facts. We must have an interpreter, and he must not only know the facts but also the meaning behind them. That interpreter is God, and the only Intepreter between God and man is Christ. He created and purposed everything. Nothing has happened that did not fit into His purpose.

There are those who believe that history can be properly interpreted through observation. They point to the evidence that any rational person would consider valid to prove the existence of God and His faithfulness. This line of thinking tends to rely solely on the prophecies that are fulfilled in such an obviously literal manner that anyone would recognize it. Though these prophecies are valid, there are many more clues that need divine revelation to make the story come out right. Israel had the observational view, but they missed the real point of the story. As a result, they rejected the Messiah who had been promised in many texts which could only be understood through revelation.

The story of history moves from partial to full, shadow to substance, and natural to spiritual. The New Testament explains in full what the Old Testament tells in part. Paul says his assignment is to make the "**word**

of God fully known." Only after the Christ-event could anyone know how history would really work out. As the gospel went from primarily Jewish disciples to primarily Gentile disciples, the mystery was still being explained, thus the letter of Paul and Peter identify the true people of God.

Is There a Central Theme?

History reveals a good God who is totally in charge. He shows His goodness in creation. He made everything that was made out of His love. He wanted a people who could enjoy His life as much as He does. He blessed the couple in the Garden with His fellowship, with the dignity to partner with Him in subduing the earth, and with the resources necessary to carry out their assignment. Later, after the fall of mankind, He revealed Himself to Abraham as the blessing God. He chose Abraham to be blessed and to be a blessing to the whole world. He blessed Abraham's offspring in various ways and finally, He blessed the world by sending God's Son and Abraham's seed, to be the Savior of all, to restore everything to its original purpose.

Another part of history's theme is that God chose to save mankind by using mankind.

Then, we could say that history reveals this sovereign, good God as one who rules by His Word. He spoke, and creation happened. He spoke, and Abraham became a nation. He spoke, and Israel became His son. He spoke through the prophets, and Israel found hope. Finally, He spoke through His Son, Jesus, and salvation appeared.

Throughout time, we see blessings evident on those who are under His Word. When His Word is neglected or rejected, the blessings cease and curses appear. At the end, we discover that it was Jesus the Word who was the agent of creation and that He is the sustainer of history. Since the Bible is the record of God's work in history through Jesus, we know it is the Word of God. Some decide whether the Bible deserves the right to be called the Word of God based on whether or not it affects their lives. Actually, it is the Word of God because of its relationship to Jesus, the ultimate and final Word of God.

Another part of history's theme is that God chose to save mankind by using mankind. He did it the only way possible to preserve His justice and mercy. He was faithful to His creation and to His covenant. He never violated the dignity of man's image, but it never got out of His control. He worked through the choices of mankind to bring mankind a Savior out of mankind, so mankind could again experience the life shared with God.

How Significant Is Israel in History?

Obviously, Israel was a major player. God chose to work through Abraham's descendants to bring the world a Savior. Abraham was not better than others. God selected him to be the servant to the world. His descendants were not better either. They were God's vessels of mercy. They would be the microcosm of humanity that God would use to bring about His redemption. For God's version of salvation to take place, there needed to be a full disclosure of the depths of sin. Then, there needed to be a substitute who would satisfy God's justice and display His mercy. It would all be done in a way that salvation would be open to everyone on the basis of faith.

God chose to work through Abraham's descendants to bring the world a Savior.

So God brought nearly two million of Abraham's descendants out of Egyptian bondage. To historical observers, this was just another event in the evolution of nations. But God explained that this event was pivotal to the purpose of history. He gave them His Law. It was good. It showed how life should be lived in covenant with God. It offered order, peace, and productivity. Israel was thrilled. God had given them something no other nation had. But here is one of the major twists in the story: They couldn't keep the Law. Only in the New Testament do we discover that God gave His Law to expose the depth of sin in mankind (see Romans 7).

Israel was the world's model. Privileged beyond all nations with the explicit laws of God, she could not keep them. All peoples had the Law written on their consciences and could see its imprint on creation, but Israel had the clear statutes written down. She failed, just as surely as any Gentile nation would have done. This failure proves that no one can be righteous by keeping the Law. Israel did the world another favor. But she was not done.

It was through the descendants of Abraham that Jesus was born. He came as the ultimate Israelite. He represented Israel as the final sin-bearer.

When He died, it was to fulfill Israel's destiny as **"the kingdom of priests" (see Exodus 19:6),** and to save all who would come to Him in faith. Even in their worst moment, when they rejected the Messiah, they were part of the human element in crucifying the Lamb of God who takes away the sin of the world. Their rejection of the Messiah opened the way for salvation to be offered to the rest of the world. If they had not rejected Him, there would have been no crucifixion and no salvation.

The necessity of Israel's failure adds another twist to the story as explained by God's revelation. If they had received the Messiah, they surely would have confused His mercy with their ethnic rights. After all they were special; they had rights to God (based on ethnicity, so they thought).

As a result of their failure, they had to realize that the Gentiles received the inheritance which they were promised. These uncircumcised Gentiles enjoyed fellowship with God. They were called His sons. They enjoyed the Spirit of God in them. They became the new kingdom of kings and priests. Israel would have to humble themselves and receive the same mercy the unqualified Gentiles received. This is how **"all Israel will be saved" (see Romans 11:26).** God's Israel has always been those who believe Him. Now He is revealing that His people are from both ethnic Israel and from non-ethnic Israel (see Galatians 3:7, 9, 14, 29, 6:16; Romans 9:6-7).

Their rejection of the Messiah opened the way for salvation to be offered to the rest of the world.

God has dealt with the sin issue that came into history through Adam. He used Adam's descendants to eliminate it. In the process, He has revealed His mercy in ways that the human mind could not envision.

> **Oh, the depth of the riches and wisdom and knowledge of God! How unsearchable are his judgments and how inscrutable his ways! (Romans 11:33 ESV)**

Now there is an Israel of God on earth to carry on the purpose of proclaiming the gospel to the world. Those who respond will be equipped to again engage in subduing the earth in partnership with God Himself. The new people of God on earth are not marked by ethnicity. They are only divided by whether they are "in Christ" or outside Christ. Ethnicity does not give advantage or disadvantage. The blessings of the sovereign, good God come on those who trust Christ alone for their righteousness. They have the Spirit of Christ to fulfill the Torah. They have the body of Christ filled with the Spirit to fulfill the need for the temple. They have the identity of being sons of God. They have the whole world as their sphere of rule instead of a small piece of land between the river and the sea. They have the renewed purpose to bless the world by presenting a Savior who died for their sins and lives for their hope. They operate under a new covenant that transforms them instead of exposing their flesh.

History has meaning. It is not left up to the observer. He or she could not interpret it without God anyway. God has devised it and carried it out. He has used time and humanity to display His glory. All along the way, we see His mercy shine. He always picks the needy. He likes to show His grace to the unqualified; therefore He has worked it so that all are in that category. That is good news to those of us who are not in the elite class. We are candidates for His mercy.

If the big story of history has meaning, then our story must have meaning. God has us where we can be a part of the purpose to bless His world through our relationship with Christ. We can accept our place and rely on mercy, or strive to gain blessings in another impossible way. Surely we have learned history's lesson that only those who live under the rule of God's Word are blessed with order, peace, and productivity. His Word today is consistent with His Word in Christ and with the record of His acts in history. He is not hesitant to speak to us, and He has given us ears to hear what He says. ■

Dudley Hall is president of Successful Christian Living Ministries, a ministry dedicated to the restoration of the individual and the church according to God's original plan. As a teacher and popular conference speaker within the body of Christ, Dudley shares the truths which God has imparted to him simply and concisely, offering practical insights to enable believers to grow in their relationships with Christ. Dudley is the author of numerous books, including: *Grace Works*, *A Treasure Worth the Effort*, and *Incense and Thunder*. He and his wife, Betsy, live in Texas with their two children: David and Karis.

Freedom Through Forgiveness

by Deborah Joyner Johnson

To be a Christian means to forgive the inexcusable because God has forgiven the inexcusable in you. —*C. S. Lewis*

Those who do great things do not allow their past failures and mistakes to stop them from moving forward. We have all sinned and fallen short at times. We may wish we could go back and change the past, but we cannot. Our minds can easily go to the place of "what ifs?" If we live in the past, we cannot proceed forward. Although we cannot change the past, we can improve the future. The way to be free of previous mistakes is to accept freedom through forgiveness.

Satan likes nothing better than to hold the past over our heads, reminding us daily of former sins. This will keep us in bondage so that our lives will go nowhere. Satan would like to see us lead guilt-ridden lives for the remainder of our time on earth. Why? He knows with guilt hanging over us, we will believe the lie that we are not worthy to accomplish anything.

Satan will also do his best to hold past sins over our heads. If we allow the enemy's guilt to control our minds, it will stop us from fulfilling our purpose in life. A close friend of mine once told me that the enemy will try to take our pasts and hold them over our heads like swords, keeping us in bondage, afraid to move. We should reach up and grab those swords and plunge them into the enemy. Our pasts are our testimonies and make us who we are. God uses everything for good. We can look at our pasts, see the working of God in all of it, and know that we have been changed for the better because of it. It is the word of our testimony that will be used to bring down the enemy in our lives and the lives of others.

Forgiveness Is the Key

By studying the life of Jesus, we can learn all there is to know about forgiveness. He forgave because of His unconditional love. He was a Shepherd to the lost, a Friend to sinners, and Healer to the sick simply because He loved them. He taught, nurtured, and loved all people—even those we might deem unlovable by our standards. No one was unlovable to Him. He came to give, never expecting anything in return. He was tortured for sins He never committed and suffered the most horrible death imaginable. Even then, in pain inconceivable, He forgave those who were putting Him to death. The very ones who were spitting, laughing, and cursing Him were the ones He was forgiving. He forgave us all for all eternity. This is the perfection of love.

You might say, "Well, that was Jesus and He was perfect. He didn't have to endure what we do in this life. How can we be expected to forgive and love as He did?" Jesus went through the same temptations and hardships that we go through in this life and yet He prevailed. We are told in Hebrews 4:15: **"For we do not have a high priest who cannot sympathize with our weaknesses, but One who has been tempted in all things as we are, yet without sin."** He suffered every temptation known to man and still did not sin. He came to earth as a man and had the same feelings that we do, yet He still forgave throughout His life.

Guilt will still have a hold on our lives if we have wronged others and have not made it right by asking forgiveness.

Forgiveness

As we confess our sins and ask forgiveness, then we are absolutely forgiven. Our sins are gone and washed by the blood of Jesus. After we have been washed clean from sin, then it is erased as though it was never there. And, the wall that has separated us from God is removed. Dwight L. Moody once said, "God has cast our confessed sins into the depths of the sea, and He's even put a 'No Fishing' sign over the spot." Psalm 103:12 states: **"As far as the east is from the west, so far has He removed our transgressions from us."** As we accept the Lord's forgiveness, our minds will be free as well—free to allow His creativity to flow within us.

Along with asking forgiveness from the Lord for our sins, if we have wronged others in the past, we need to ask their forgiveness as well. Guilt will still have a hold on our lives if we have wronged others and have not made it right by asking forgiveness. They may or may not forgive you, but that is not your dilemma—it is theirs. Once you have asked forgiveness, you will find new freedom in your life.

There is one more step to forgiveness—we must forgive those who have wronged us. This becomes a little more difficult, especially if wounds have developed from hurts and abuse. As we forgive others, we will be completely free and healed. Otherwise the roots of bitterness, rejection, and so on will still have their hold on us, plaguing our minds. How many times should we forgive someone? Jesus gave us the answer.

> **Then Peter came and said to Him, "Lord, how often shall my brother sin against me and I forgive him? Up to seven times?"**
>
> **Jesus said to him, "I do not say to you, up to seven times, but up to seventy times seven" (Matthew 18:21-22).**

Jesus knows how hard this life is and He even sympathizes with us. He will also help us as Hebrews 4:16 states. **"Therefore let us draw near with confidence to the throne of grace, so that we may receive mercy and find grace to help in time of need."** I have found that by asking the Lord to let me see others through His eyes and feel His compassion, I am able to forgive them. It feels like a cloud has been removed and finally I can see who that person really is. If we ask, He will be faithful to show us why His love is so great for that person. By spending time with the Lord, who is Love, we will become more like Him and take on His characteristics. Receiving His love will enable us to have love for others and forgive them.

As we forgive others, we will be completely free and healed.

Paul tells us in II Corinthians 5:14: **"for the love of Christ controls us...."** If His love controlled us, then we would be able to love and forgive as Jesus does. To love, we must die—die to selfish feelings, anger, resentment, bitterness, and discontentment. We must die to those feelings of hurt, turn the other cheek, forgive, and love unconditionally. Solomon tells us in Proverbs 10:12 that **"Hatred stirs up strife, but love covers all transgressions."** If we love, we can forgive trespasses against us.

When we no longer think about how a person has wronged us, we know we have truly forgiven because the wrongs are no longer consuming our thoughts. If we can learn to live with love as our guide, it will not be so difficult to forgive. To be Christlike, we have to forgive. As we forgive those who mistreat us, the enemy no longer has any power over us in that area. The blood of Jesus breaks that power and we are set free—free to let go of the past and spring forward into the future. The feeling will be much the same as being set free from prison. The confining walls will be knocked down and we will be able to walk forward with true freedom. When the guilt and condemnation of our old issues no longer control us, we can take a quantum leap into freedom, and it is a wonderful feeling.

Every day is a new day, full of new possibilities. When we ask forgiveness from the Lord, ask forgiveness from those we have wronged, and forgive those who have wronged us, we will be set free. We will be more free than we have ever experienced. Living water will then begin to wash through us, releasing pent-up creativity within us. As we live in this realm of having a clean slate daily, His love will be the guide to fulfilling all that we have been called to do.

We do not know how much time we have on the earth, but as we wake up each day, we have another chance to fulfill that which we have been called to do. Take this new day as a gift from the Lord. ■

> *The greatest thing is to be found at one's post as a child of God, living each day as though it were our last, but planning as though our world might last a hundred years.* —*C. S. Lewis*

This article is an excerpt from the chapter titled, Victory Over Guilt, in Deborah's book, Pathway to Purpose. *This book is available through our website: www.MorningStarMinistries.org or by calling 1-800-542-0278.*

Deborah Joyner Johnson is the managing editor for MorningStar Publications and Ministries. Deborah writes articles for *The Morning Star Journal* and has published two books, *The Chosen Path* and *Pathway to Purpose*. She has a gifted teaching ministry and shares at conferences and women's groups. Deborah lives in North Carolina and has three children: Matthew, Meredith, and Abby.

Justice, Law, and Legalism—Part I

by An Orthodox Jewish Rabbi

In discussing the subject of justice within the body of Christ, I have had numerous people say to me something along the lines that it is not justice they want, but grace. I have even had a few people ask me directly to help them find biblical evidence that justice is the opposite of God's grace. This speaks of a profound misunderstanding of what justice is. Somewhere over the course of time since the Reformation, some have overreacted so much to the problem of legalism that they now look upon any form of law or guiding principle as the opposite of God's intent. I hope to be able to demonstrate here that a proper understanding of justice is as important as an understanding of grace.

The Scripture states, **"Righteousness and justice are the foundation of thy throne of God" (see Psalm 89:14).** To start from the beginning, we have to look into what a throne is and why it matters where God sits. In Jewish tradition and thought, the throne of God symbolizes God's interaction with the world and His people. You will notice that in the inaugural visions of the major prophets, Isaiah, Jeremiah, and Ezekiel, as well as in the Book of Revelation, each of the interactive visions start with a throne vision. To give imagery, in ancient times, when a king would receive people, even his dearest friends, he would come out and sit on his throne. That being the case, for God to have full involvement with His people, righteousness and justice must be present.

A throne is also a symbol of rulership. The throne is the symbol of authority that a king holds. If God is to be our King, He must have a throne upon which to sit. He must have a place of authority within our midst. However, if we cut justice out of the mix we undermine that place of authority. The foundation of the throne can be compared to the legs of a chair—if you take off two legs from any chair, you make it impossible to sit in. To the extent that we remove either righteousness or justice from our lives and from our communities, in equal proportion we will undermine and destroy the foundation of our relationship with God. To that extent, we will remove from our midst a place suitable to the Lord. God cannot be the King of our hearts and our lives if He cannot sit upon the throne of His rulership because we have knocked the foundation out from under it.

Not only is it necessary for both righteousness and justice to be present in order for there to be a proper foundation, but in truth you cannot have one without the other. Righteousness and justice are in fact two different sides to the same coin. Without justice, there is no standard by which we can measure righteousness. There is nothing to tell us when we have gone off the path of proper living. At the same time, without righteousness all justice will ultimately be perverted. It does not matter how perfect the system is; if the people behind it are hedonistic sinners, it will be a perverted system serving their wants and lusts. One need only look to Jesus' trial to see this. I have no doubts that the system of justice which God commanded Israel, and carried through into the New Testament, was a perfect system. However, when wicked men hijacked it, they perverted that perfect system to the point where they actually put its Creator on the cross.

Without justice, there is no standard by which we can measure righteousness.

We must define what justice is. We can throw around terms, but if we each still have our own preconceived notions of what something means, it does not help with understanding. On a very basic level, a system of justice in any secular government is primarily in place to protect the rights and privileges of its citizens. In the kingdom of God, justice is also supposed to be a protection of the rights of the citizenry. The purpose of justice within the kingdom is to ensure that each child of God receives every right and ounce of benefit for which the Lord Jesus Christ died. In order to accomplish this, the system of justice in the kingdom, much like in our secular justice systems, is supposed to set the law and standard of living and relating to one another.

The word "law" above is not an error, nor is it a typo. Law is a part of justice. Law is necessary for life; without law there is not a standard by which we live. Most importantly though, law does not equal legalism; law and legalism are not the same thing. For instance, on every blow-dryer there is a label stating quite explicitly not to use that blow-dryer while taking a bath. We look at such labels as common sense, but if it were common sense, they would not need to put it there. Disobeying the label also does not necessarily affect your relationship with the Lord. It may qualify you for a Darwin award; it may even bring you into a literal face-to-face relationship with God, but in truth, the law is there to warn you about the consequences of inappropriate behavior. I personally do not know of anyone who reads one of these restrictions on a blow-dryer and then complains that the company who made it is being legalistic.

The same can be said of DUI (driving under the influence of alcohol and/or drugs) laws which each state and country have enacted. These laws are there for the protection of every citizen. If a person is impaired, driving a vehicle simply is not safe, and those who do so, if not stopped, in many cases end up hurting or killing an innocent person. Again, when most people read or hear about the DUI laws of their locality, they do not complain that their state is being legalistic—most quietly thank God that someone has had the good sense to watch over the safety of the general public. There are those who do complain, but in my experience most of them live in a state of lawlessness which disregards those around them for the sake of their own pleasures. I will write more about this in a moment, but for now I want to stay concentrated on the idea that law is not legalism.

These laws are there for the protection of every citizen.

Law, taken within the proper context, is a system of guidelines which enables us to love God and to love our neighbors in a way that will not damage them or us. There is a story in the Talmud[1] that depicts this dichotomy between law and legalism well. A pagan became interested in Judaism, so he went to a great rabbi named Shammai[2] and said, "Teach me the entire law while standing on one foot." Shammai grew angry

[1] Shabbat 31a

[2] One of the two greatest rabbis of his generation.

and said it was impossible—there are 613 commandments in the Torah[3] and each must be learned and mastered with all of its derivations before one can begin to understand and live the law. So the pagan went away. Eventually, this same pagan came to Hillel[4] and made the same request of him. Hillel without hesitating stood on one foot and said, **"And you shall love the LORD your God with all your heart and with all your soul and with all your might" (Deuteronomy 6:5)**, and **"you shall love your neighbor as yourself" (see Leviticus 19:18);** the rest is commentary, go and learn." On account of this answer, the pagan was converted to Judaism.

This is the prime difference between a proper relationship with and understanding of law and legalism. Law in its proper context gives us an understanding of how to either love and serve God or how to love and properly treat your neighbor. Thus was Hillel able to say that the other 611 commandments were nothing more than commentary on these two. To Shammai, the legalist, this was not good enough. For him, the law was not a means to an end, but both the means and the end. For him, the law had become an idol that so consumed him that he allowed it to block others from coming into a loving relationship with God. While law creates healthy boundaries that enable relationships, legalism causes distance which disables relationships.

While law creates healthy boundaries that enable relationships, legalism causes distance which disables relationships.

Within legalism there is no room for love or for forgiveness. Legalism requires strict adherence to the rules and the imputation of guilt for the slightest infraction. The Book of Hebrews 9:8-10 states, **"The Holy Spirit is signifying this, that the way into the holy place has not yet been disclosed, while the outer tabernacle is still standing, which**

[3] There are, when counted, 613 specific commandments throughout the five books of Moses that God specifically commanded Israel. Then from the beginning of the Rabbinic period in Nehemiah's time the rabbis began to interpret and explain each of these commandments and their specific applications. This interpretation eventually turned into the Talmud, a 30,000 page document.

[4] The other great rabbi of his generation, as well as the grandfather and one of the two teachers of Gamaliel, Paul's teacher.

is a symbol for the present time. Accordingly both gifts and sacrifices are offered which cannot make the worshiper perfect in conscience, since they relate only to food and drink and various washings, regulations for the body imposed until a time of reformation." Notice the passage does not say that these sacrifices are unable to make a person right in the eyes of God, but rather within their own minds and consciences they still feel their guilt. The reason for this is not the imperfection of the system which God laid down, but rather it is the rational end of a system which descended into legalism. Once legalism was allowed in the door, simple items of food, some spilled wine, or a dip in mikvah[5] is not capable of rectifying the breaking of a commandment because it cannot undo that which has been done, and legalism does not allow for forgiveness and grace. Even though the Law which God laid down makes provision for His forgiveness and grace to minister to the human lost condition, legalism excised it out.

It is important to note that just because we have faith in Jesus Christ, this does not make us free from legalism.

It is important to note that just because we have faith in Jesus Christ, this does not make us free from legalism. I was once attending an inner healing class put on by a fairly famous inner healing ministry. They were lecturing on helping people get forgiveness for past, unrepented sins, and in this process they spoke about theft. The leader of this organization made a statement that God could not forgive a person until they had made restitution, even if the sin was committed before the person was Christian. I did not take this well, and made quite a vocal protest. Essentially, I felt then and still believe now they were stating that the blood of Christ was insufficient to cover this sin. This person and others there made the point that I was a rabbi and thus should be in full favor of this. My reply was simple; early on in the rediscovery of my Jewish roots, I descended into legalism, and while free of it now, as a repentant legalist I am familiar with that

[5] A type of Jewish baptismal used for cleansing impurity.

spirit—we can smell our own. Legalism will always take law and make it a thing that must be done in order to be acceptable to God, instead of what should be done to please God.

Legalism promotes idolization of law, but prevents and blocks wholesome and healthy relationships. Law on the other hand, when used as a means with a spirit of love, creates healthy boundaries which lead to healthy relationships. For instance, in my marriage there are rules—laws, if you will, that guide the way my wife and I relate to one another. Some of these rules are things such as we do not seek romantic relationships with other people. We do not strike one another. We speak to each other with respect and treat each other with respect. These rules should be a part of every relationship. Again, healthy individuals would not see these as legalistic rules, but good advice for a lasting marriage. Far from locking us into a system of death that blocks a true relationship of love and trust from developing, these rules establish the necessary healthy boundaries that ensure not only the development of a loving relationship, but also the continued life and growth of our relationship.

Our purpose in life should be to grow closer to the Lord and to grow in love.

In truth, God's Law works the same way. Paul, the man so often quoted as being anti-law, himself states, **"Therefore the Law has become our tutor to lead us to Christ, that we may be justified by faith" (Galatians 3:24).** Notice the law is not the end, it is not the goal, but rather it leads us to the goal. Just as maps and road signs help us plan a trip and then stay on the proper route by pointing us in the right direction, so, too, is the purpose of the Law. We do not go on a road trip for the sake of the map, and we do not go on a road trip for the sake of the road signs—we go on the road trip for the purpose of reaching a certain destination. So, too, our purpose in life should be to grow closer to the Lord and to grow in love. God's commandments, His Law, then are not the purpose for the journey, but they are the map and signs along the way that let us know that we are still on the proper path and headed in the right direction. Just as the signs are the means and not the end, so the Law has to be the means and never the end.

This idea is even evidenced within the order of events in Scripture. Most commonly, when we think of Law, we think of the Torah that God gave the Israelites through Moses. The interesting thing is that the covenant was not based upon that Law—at least it was not supposed to be. The covenant may have been twisted into legalism, but initially the covenant was supposed to be based on God's redemption in bringing the Jewish people out of Egypt. So much so that when God began giving the Jewish people the Law through the discourse often called the "ten commandments" He stated, **"I am the Lord your God, who brought you out of the land of Egypt, out of the house of slavery" (Exodus 20:2).** This was the very first commandment. In fact, the formula **"I am the Lord your God, who brought you out of Egypt"** is used more than 150 times throughout the Torah by God as the reason why the Israelites should obey whatever commandment He is giving them at the time. The point seems to be clear: God is not so much demanding that the people follow commandments as much as He is asking them to respond in kind on account of the great work He has done on their behalf.

Initially the covenant was supposed to be based on God's redemption in bringing the Jewish people out of Egypt.

The same is true of the New Covenant. Long before Paul or any other apostle wrote a single letter commanding believers to act according to certain principles, Jesus first laid down His life for man for us to attain perfection in God's sight through His own sacrifice. Only then do we begin to receive the instruction of the New Testament, and even there I would argue that the language is the same. As Paul writes, **"Therefore, I urge you, brothers, in view of God's mercy, to offer your bodies as living sacrifices, holy and pleasing to God—this is your spiritual act of worship" (Romans 12:1 NIV).** Here, too, Paul is telling us not to seek relationship with God through our deeds, but rather to respond to God's love for us with deeds. By always viewing our works as a response to the incredible goodness of God, we will prevent ourselves from being deceived into thinking that it is through the merit of our deeds that we draw closer to Him. Having laid down His life for us, I do believe that Jesus deserves our very best in return.

Often I have seen the New Testament held up against the Old Testament as grace versus Law. I do not think that God's overall message has changed that much over time. Yes, we do have a better covenant; but a covenant has always been by His grace. Even the New Testament is not devoid of commandments. I had a Jewish friend who was once having a Bible study for a group of Christians. He decided to have them go through the New Testament and list, categorize, and count each commandment given through the New Testament. He called me one day very excited; apparently his group had counted over nine hundred individual commandments throughout the New Testament, and he was very happy that "they have more than us." I told him in fairly blunt terms that this was far from the brightest idea he had ever had. However, the point stands: If you want to find commandments, they can be found even in the New Testament.

Having laid down His life for us, I do believe that Jesus deserves our very best in return.

This may come as a surprise, but even though I am a rabbi and live by the Mosaic Law myself, I am absolutely not advocating that Christians even think of taking upon themselves the Laws of the Old Covenant. For that matter, I am also absolutely opposed to believers blindly following the rules laid down in the New Testament as an unbending law. Rather, I am advocating the use of the rules laid down in the New Testament to guide us in our relationships with God and with each other.

There were instances in my life where I think the difference between legalism and Law really struck home to the greatest extent. I was in a synagogue one day and there was a visiting rabbi. During the confessional section of the prayer service, he began uncontrollably weeping. After the service I asked him what was wrong. He told me that once, a couple of years ago, he had drunk a non-kosher drink by accident, and was thus attempting to atone for that accidental transgression—that he was trying to abolish the separation that it caused between him and God.

Compare that to another situation I experienced. I have a friend who is a rabbi. He called me one day saying that he needed some help at his house and would give me no more details over the phone. When I got to his house, I could tell that he was rather agitated and more than a little embarrassed, so I asked him what was going on. As it turns out he and his wife, because of a change of ingredients in a product they used in their kitchen, had been violating one of the major kosher laws for just over a year, and now the kitchen needed to be made kosher again. My mind was brought back to the scene at the synagogue where the man was weeping so bitterly over one small, accidental mistake; I could not imagine what the fallout from this would be. So I asked my friend what he was going to do, and his answer set me back as much as the one I had received at the synagogue. He said he needed to get new plates[6] and try harder to not do it again.

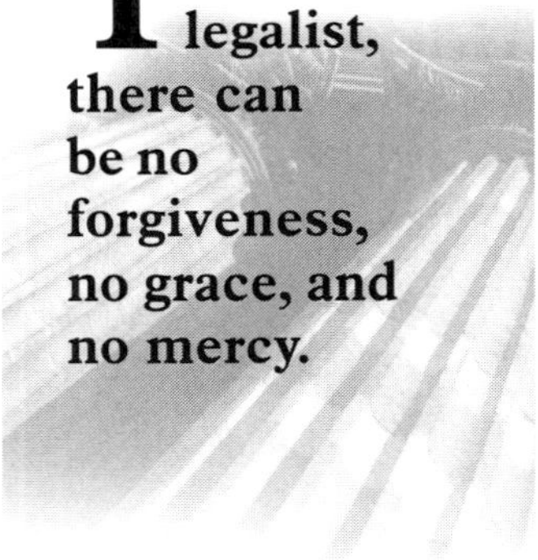

To a legalist, there can be no forgiveness, no grace, and no mercy.

I was quite struck by that statement; in fact it shocked me as much as the visiting rabbi at the synagogue. To me, the two together gave a good picture of the difference between legalism and Law. To a legalist, there can be no forgiveness, no grace, and no mercy. A violation of a rule drives a wedge into the relationship that cannot be easily removed, and in some cases may never be removed, if only on a subconscious level. However, to one whom the Law is as it was always intended to be—guidelines for righteous living, the answer is simple. Make your apologies and move on—hopefully learning from your own mistakes.

As I thought about this, another realization struck me. Long before God gave Israel the Law at Mount Sinai, He first delivered them from

[6] Because the old ones were no longer kosher (fitting for Jewish dietary law).

Egypt. His salvation from the house of bondage was not conditional on Israel's keeping His Law, but rather on His grace alone. In the same way, long before a single pen stroke of the New Testament ever made it to paper, Jesus laid down His life to free us all from our spiritual bondage. In both cases, the many writings and rules which may have followed were given to be a response, a way of living uprightly and in appropriate response to the grace and mercy that the Lord of all had already shown those that He chose to be His people.

Legalism implies that we need to do something in order to be acceptable to God that we need to live in a certain way in order to be brought near to God. Stated simply, that is a denial of the finished work of the cross. Christ, through His death, brought us as close to God as we are ever going to get. All that remains is our own unbelief. It is our unbelief and our inability to acknowledge and accept such love that brings us to a place where we seek a form of legalism as the answer. If, however, we can set aside our own unbelief and simply accept the love that God has shown us, then we will see the rules for what they truly are, a means of living a life worthy of our calling (see Ephesians 4:1).

Legalism implies that we need to do something in order to be acceptable to God.

Paul writes concerning the Law, **"Love is the fulfillment of the law" (see Romans 13:10 NIV).** Love sums up God's law; it is just that simple. There is a reason that when Jesus was questioned as to the greatest commandment He said, **"The foremost is, 'Hear, O Israel! The Lord our God is one Lord; and you shall love the Lord your God with all your heart, and with all your soul, and with all your mind, and with all your strength.' The second is this, 'You shall love your neighbor as yourself.' There is no other commandment greater than these" (Mark 12:29-31).** If we truly love God and love man, and are in perfect relationship, embodying perfect love, rules are unnecessary. Rules are only necessary for those of us (myself the chief amongst them) who have not yet attained to perfect love. Until that love is perfected, rules are necessary to keep us from doing harm to those with whom we have relationship.

Relationship with God in many ways can be compared to a marriage. The longer I am married to my wife, the more I instinctively know what makes her happy and what will hurt her feelings. Thus, loving my wife, the longer we are married, the more these things become instinctual, and the less I need her to tell me what to do and what not do. In the same way, God's rules are to help keep us from hurting God's heart and from hurting those around us. The longer we are in relationship with Him, the less we will need to have those things spelled out for us.

One of the things which justice does in God's system is to help enforce these rules, especially between the brethren, thus ensuring that should love fail, the children of God would be protected from those who would do them harm. Also, it is a means to heal those relationships which may have been harmed on account of such a failing. It is this upholding of the rules that God has laid down for relationships between the brethren and with other people for which justice is best known. However, justice is far more than law; it is much more than enforcing rules or regulations. In its proper context, justice also means loving our neighbors, here and abroad. ■

My great concern is not whether you have failed, but whether you are content with your failure.

—Abraham Lincoln

Mustard Seeds of Wisdom

The
OVERCOMING LIFE
Truth for a Victorious Life

The Stronghold of Christ's Likeness

by Francis Frangipane

Victory begins with the name of Jesus on our lips. It is consummated by the nature of Jesus in our hearts.

God's Highest Purpose

Most Christians only engage in spiritual warfare with a hope of either relieving present distresses or attaining a "normal" existence. However, the purpose of all aspects of spirituality, warfare included, is to bring us into the image of Christ. Nothing, not worship nor warfare, neither love nor deliverance, is truly attainable if we miss the singular objective of our faith: Christlikeness.

Let us recall that the Lord delivered the ancient Hebrews out of Egypt so He could bring them into the Promised Land. Likewise, we are delivered out of sin, not that we might live for ourselves, but that we might come into Christlikeness. Our goals must align with God's, for if our nature does not change, we will invariably find ourselves entangled in the same problems that caused our difficulties in the first place.

For this reason, many of our spiritual conflicts simply are not going to cease until the character of the Lord Jesus is formed in our hearts. The Father's goal in deliverance is much more than simply seeing our burdens or the devil taken off our backs. Indeed, the specific purpose toward which God steers the working of all things in our lives is our conformity "to the image of His Son." The Father's purpose in our salvation was that Jesus would become **"the first born among many brethren" (see Romans 8:29).** In other words, the way to realize God's ultimate victory is to reach toward His ultimate goal, which is complete transformation into the likeness of Christ.

There is an interpenetration of spirit between God and ourselves where our spirits are fully saturated with the living presence of the Lord Jesus, where His glory so floods our lives that there is **"no dark part"** left within us (see Luke 11:36). This immediacy of the Lord's presence produces an indestructible defense, a fortress within which we are hidden from evil. Through Him, we enter the excellence of His ways in our relationships both with the Father and one another, thereby walking in immunity from countless satanic attacks. Indeed, as His fullness within us increases, that which is written is fulfilled: **"As He is, so also are we in this world"** and **"He who was born of God keeps** [us] **and the evil one does not touch** [us]" **(see I John 4:17, 5:18).**

We must realize that it is not Satan who defeats us; it is our openness to him. To perfectly subdue the devil, we must walk in the **"shelter of the Most High" (see Psalm 91:1).** Satan is tolerated for one purpose: The warfare between the devil and God's saints thrusts us into Christlikeness, where the nature of Christ becomes our only place of rest and security. God allows warfare to facilitate His eternal plan, which is to make man in His image (see Genesis 1:26).

Once we realize that the Father's goal is to transform our lives, we will continually find that God has one answer to spiritual warfare: Appropriate the nature of His Son! Are you troubled by demons of fear or doubt? Submit those areas to God, repenting of your unbelief, and then yield yourself to Christ's faith within you. Are you troubled with spirits of lust and shame? Present those very areas of sin to God, repenting of your old nature, drawing upon the forgiveness of Christ and His purity of heart.

The Father is more concerned with the coming forth of His Son in our lives than He is with defeating Satan. Who is the devil, that he can defy the living God? Indeed, it is of the greatest truth that once the devil recognizes that his assault against your life has not pulled you from God, but toward Him—once he perceives that his temptations are actually forcing you to appropriate the virtue of Christ—the enemy will withdraw.

The Goal Is Christlikeness, Not Warfare

There will come a time when the Lord will lead us to confront the strongholds of hell over our churches and our communities. There are other times however, that to engage in much spiritual warfare is actually a distraction from your obedience to God. Jesus defeated Satan in Gethsemane and at the cross, not by directly confronting the devil but by fulfilling the destiny to which He had been called at Calvary. The greatest battle that was ever won was accomplished by the apparent death of the victor, without even a word of rebuke to His adversary. The prince of this world was judged and principalities and powers were disarmed not by confrontational warfare, but by the surrender of Jesus Christ on the cross.

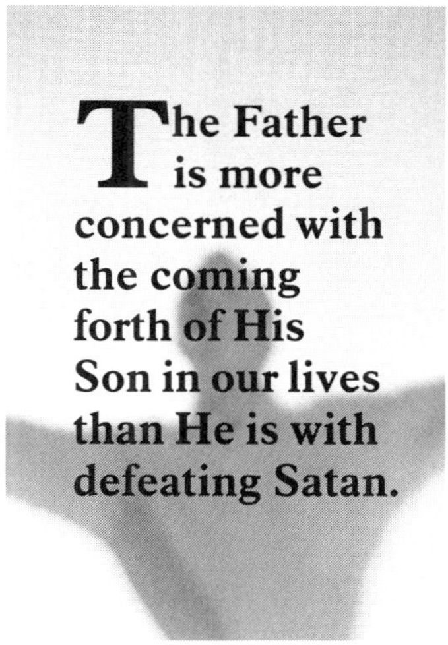

There are occasions when your battle against the devil is actually a digression from the higher purpose that God has for you. Intercessors and warfare leaders take note: There is a demon whose purpose is to lure one's mind into hell. If we were to name this spirit, we would call it "Wrong Focus." You may be fighting this very spirit if you are continually seeing evil spirits in people or in the material world around you. The ultimate goal of this demon is to produce mental illness in saints who move in deliverance. We are not called to focus on the battle or the devil, except when that battle hinders our immediate transformation into Christ's likeness. Our calling is to focus on Jesus. The work of the devil, however, is to draw our eyes from Jesus. Satan's first weapon always involves luring our eyes from Christ. Turn toward Jesus and almost immediately the battle vanishes.

I knew a man once who owned a record company. Besides running the operation, he also spent many hours in production listening to the "mother disk," which was the master from which all subsequent recordings were produced. Over the years, his ears became adept at catching the "pops and sizzles"—the imperfections that had to be eliminated in the master. I remarked one day that I thought working with music must be enjoyable. His response was enlightening. He said, "You know, I haven't listened to music in years. When I turn on my sophisticated home stereo, no matter what recording I'm listening to, all I hear are the pops and sizzles."

In the same way his thoughts were bent toward musical imperfections, so wrong focus will seek to turn your thoughts continually toward the enemy. Suddenly, all you will see are demons. The true gift called "discerning of spirits" is a balanced gift which enables you to recognize at least as many angelic spirits as you do evil spirits. The proper manifestation of this gift has a much more positive focus and influence than what commonly masquerades as discernment.

An example of the proper balance in discernment is seen in II Kings. The Syrian army had surrounded Dothan, a city in Israel, much to the consternation of the Prophet Elisha's servant. To calm his attendant's fright, Elisha prayed that his servant's eyes would be opened. He then encouraged his servant, saying, **"Do not fear, for those who are with us are more than those who are with them" (see II Kings 6:16).** As the Lord opened the servant's eyes, he saw what Elisha saw: **"The mountain was full of horses and chariots of fire all around Elisha" (v. 17).**

In spiritual warfare, the battle is never limited to an "us against them" human affair. It always includes "those with us" against "those with them." True discernment is as fully aware of the vast multitude of angels loyal to God as it is aware of the activity of the demonic realm—and it is aware that the angelic hosts on our side are both stronger and more numerous than the enemy. Remember, if you fail to "hear the music" in your times of warfare, your discernment is incomplete.

We must learn that, on a personal level, it is better to develop godly virtues than to spend our day praying against the devil. Indeed, it is the joy of the Lord that casts out spirits of depression. It is our living faith which destroys spirits of unbelief; it is aggressive love which casts out fear.

As we continually yield ourselves to Christ, surrendering ourselves by faith to His nature and His words, we literally build the impenetrable stronghold of His presence around us. The way into the fortress of the Almighty is simple. Victory begins with the name of Jesus on our lips. It is consummated by the nature of Jesus in our hearts. ■

Excerpted from The Three Battlegrounds, *Arrow Publications, 2006 edition,* www.arrowbookstore.com

---

Francis Frangipane is the senior pastor of River of Life Ministries in Cedar Rapids, Iowa, and the president of Advancing Church Ministries. The Lord has used Francis to unite thousands of pastors in prayer in hundreds of cities. With more than a million copies of his best-selling books in print, and with an expanding radio and television ministry called "In Christ's Image," Francis is in much demand worldwide. His newest book is entitled, *This Day We Fight!* For more information, visit: www.InChristsImage.org.

The Gospel Truth

by Rick Joyner

When Napoleon read the Gospel of John near the end of his life, he reportedly said, "Either Jesus is the Son of God or the one who wrote this gospel is! I know men, and no man could have made up a story like this." We must concur—there has never been a story written or dreamed like this one. However, it is not a story. Not only is this the greatest fact of history, it is actually the most verified act of history, with the evidence of it permeating the entire earth.

The majesty, wonder, and glory of the greatest of all miracles—God becoming a man and living among His own creation—will forever be the greatest of all miracles. God has done many great things throughout history to reveal Himself and His purpose to lead mankind and the earth back to reconciliation with Him, but none can compare to the miracle of God coming and living among us. How can we not stand in continual awe of this?

In fact, to the degree that we see this truth, our lives will be filled with awe and wonder, at everything! It is the awe and wonder that He is still here, and not only walking among us, but living in us! This miracle of God becoming a man began the greatest of all adventures, the birthing of a new creation that would span the gulf between the spiritual and natural realms.

As we proceed toward the end of this age, this bridge between the heavenly and natural realms will be found by more and more people, and the supernatural will become more and more natural to all who believe in Him. However, our goal is not to just live in the supernatural, but to live in Him. God is Spirit and those who worship Him must worship Him in Spirit and Truth. This greatest of all miracles is a miracle: Not only is the foundation of our faith supernatural, but the true Christian walk is supernatural. To say it again, it is intended to be a bridge between the spiritual and natural realms.

I love the Gospels, and read them over and over at least once a year. It is hard to fathom what Mary, the mother of Jesus, the other women who followed Him, and John, His beloved disciple, must have gone through when they had to stand there and watch the One they loved so much be tortured. But even more than this, what was it like for the Father to watch this happen to His beloved Son? I once had a prophetic experience in which I beheld the cross. I knew it was just an experience, but it was too much for me to bear. Years after this experience, I am still in awe at the strength of the women and John, and of course the love of the Father, to watch Jesus endure the real cross. It was because of love that Jesus Himself endured it.

After my experience of beholding the cross, I never wanted to see it again, and at the same time I wanted to see it again more than anything. The cross is eternal. I love the prophetic, and I love seeing things in the future, but I have always been drawn even more to seeing and understanding the past, especially the time when Jesus walked the earth.

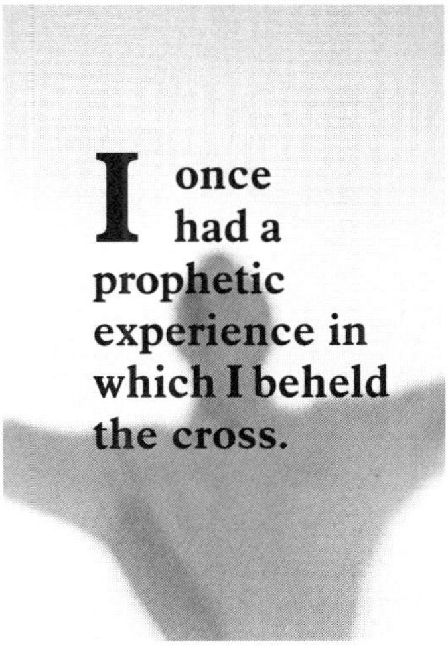

I know that the resurrected Christ dwells in unapproachable light and glory that is far more awesome than we can even comprehend or behold in these earthly bodies. He is no longer Jesus of Nazareth, but He is the Lord of glory above all rule, authority, dominion, and power. Even so, there is something about the life He lived on earth and the cross He endured that will forever be the greatest revelation of His nature—who He is. The ultimate goal of seeing what He did is to relate to Him now, who He is, and where He sits.

The "real world" is the spiritual realm, not the earthly. This realm is called but "a shadow" of the spiritual in the Scriptures, and that is indeed what it is. If we really believe the Bible, we do not just believe that all of the recorded events in it happened, though that is important, but we believe God to see the same things happen in our own lives. That is true faith in God and the Bible. Understandably, this greatest of all events, God becoming a Man and living among His own, was to compel us to live the way that He lived.

How can we live the way that Jesus lived? Of course, He lived a life of truth with a holy devotion to doing His Father's will. We might translate "holy" as being "wholly" His. Jesus has given us the same Spirit by which He did His works. His Spirit will lead us to Him and convict us when we depart from Him. His Spirit will grow His character in our lives, and give us the power to do the same works that He did. This one truth will keep us on the path of life and will always lead us to victory—it is all about Jesus. It is seeing Him, knowing Him, following Him, becoming like Him, and doing the works that He did. That is our ultimate purpose in this life, and everything else that happens in our lives is meant to help bring this to pass.

If we are growing in our purpose, we cannot help but to have an increasing devotion to a greater understanding of the greatest of all events—how God became a Man and lived upon the earth, and how He is still becoming a Man, and still walking on the earth—through us. He still seeks to do the same works that He did when He walked the earth, through us. Before the end of this age, there will be a people who will walk the earth just like Jesus did and do the works that He did—even greater works, because He now sits at the right hand of God and has sent His own Holy Spirit to be in those who follow Him.

The glory of God is about much more than just beautiful colors or heavenly music—it is His nature. King David wrote that the Lord showed His acts to the children of Israel, but to Moses He revealed His ways (see Psalm 103:7). I make no apology for the fact that I love to see the works of God, especially miracles, but it is a far greater treasure to know His ways—why He does the works that He does. This is the highest quest of man—to know the Lord and His ways and to be in unity with Him so that He can use us to do His works.

As we get closer to the end of this age and the dawning of the age in which the Lord Himself will take His authority and rule over the earth, this bridge between the spiritual and natural realms will become an essential and vital truth for the very survival of Christians. We do not war against flesh and blood, but it is a spiritual battle against spiritual powers, and we must understand this if we are going to prevail in this battle. We have been given divinely powerful, spiritual weapons as Christians.

The Bridge Between the Earthly and Heavenly

We are not alone in our journey and quest to serve the Lord, or in this battle between light and darkness. We are actually in partnership with angelic majesties whose purpose is to minister to the heirs of salvation. The New Testament encourages us to understand angels, as well as to recognize them, and even at times show them hospitality just as many of the Old Testament saints did. Showing hospitality to angels is not just to entertain them, but it is to further establish our partnership with them in the purposes of the Lord on this earth.

The Lord loves His angels too, and they love Him and us. They, too, have a great part in His plan, and though it is not our place at this time to be overly concerned about that, we do need to understand our partnership better. It is a part of building the bridge between the natural and heavenly realms. The building of this bridge was a basic purpose of Jesus, as He explained in John 1:48-51 when He first addressed Nathanael:

> **Nathanael said to Him, "How do You know me?" Jesus answered and said to him, "Before Philip called you, when you were under the fig tree, I saw you."**

Nathanael answered Him, "Rabbi, You are the Son of God; You are the King of Israel."

Jesus answered and said to him, "Because I said to you that I saw you under the fig tree, do you believe? You shall see greater things than these."

And He said to him, "Truly, truly, I say to you, you shall see the heavens opened, and the angels of God ascending and descending on the Son of Man."

By this Jesus was declaring Himself to be "Jacob's ladder." Remember when Jacob was fleeing from his brother and he laid down to sleep and had a dream of a ladder reaching into heaven? The angels of God were ascending and descending upon it, and then He saw the Lord at the top of the ladder. The Lord declared to Jacob the same promise that He had given to Abraham and Isaac. When Jacob woke up from this dream, this is what he said:

Jacob declared a truth here about the house of God which will become an increasing reality in these times.

Then Jacob awoke from his sleep and said, "Surely the Lord is in this place, and I did not know it."

And he was afraid and said, "How awesome is this place! This is none other than the house of God, and this is the gate of heaven" (Genesis 28:16-17).

Jacob declared a truth here about the house of God which will become an increasing reality in these times. The house of God is **"the gate of heaven."** The house of God, the church, is called to be the gate of heaven where the messengers of God ascend into the heavenly realm and descend back to the earth with evidence of heaven's reality. That is what Jesus was and did His whole time on the earth, and that is what He wants to do through His people now. As we are told in Revelation 4:1:

After these things I looked, and behold, a door standing open in heaven, and the first voice which I had heard, like the

sound of a trumpet speaking with me, said, "Come up here, and I will show you what must take place after these things."

This door is still open. The Lord is still beckoning us to come up to where He sits and to sit with Him. The true Christian life should lead to where we are more at home in the spiritual realm than we are in the natural. We should see more clearly with our spiritual eyes, the "eyes of our hearts," than we do with our natural eyes. True Christianity is supernatural because we are called to worship God who is Spirit, and those who worship Him must worship Him in Spirit and in Truth.

THE COMING SUPERNATURAL CHRISTIANS

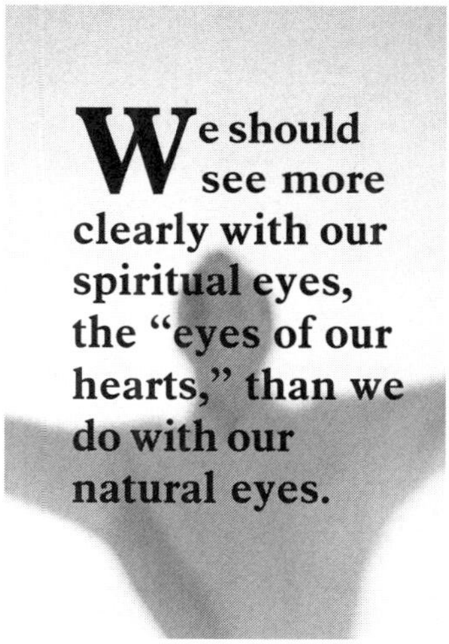

During times of great moves of God on the earth, the appearance of angels to humans inevitably increases. However, this is not as much because they are entering our realm as it is the result of people beginning to enter their realm—the spiritual realm. Being able to enter the spiritual realm should be as normal to Christians as entering their homes, because we should actually be more at home in the spiritual realm than we are in the natural. This will become an increasing reality to Christians as we come closer to the end of this age, as the sure prophecy of Scripture declares in Acts 2:17-18, which is a quote from Joel 2:

> **"And it shall come to pass in the last days, says God, that I will pour out of My Spirit on all flesh; your sons and your daughters shall prophesy, your young men shall see visions, your old men shall dream dreams.**
>
> **"And on My menservants and on My maidservants I will pour out My Spirit in those days; and they shall prophesy" (NKJV).**

Here we are told that **"in the last days"** these prophetic experiences, dreams, visions, and prophecies, will be for old and young, males and females. So as we get closer to the end of this age, we can expect these to increase, and they are. This is one of the signs that we are in the last days.

We also see in this text that these prophetic experiences are the result of the Holy Spirit being poured out. Prophetic experiences are actually one of the most sure signs of a true outpouring of the Holy Spirit. One of the results of being touched by the Holy Spirit is that He begins to open the eyes of our hearts, or our spiritual eyes, so that we begin to see into the spiritual realm. This is the basic nature of those who are born again into the new creation; they begin to see the kingdom of God. As the Lord explained before Pilate, His kingdom is not of this world or this realm.

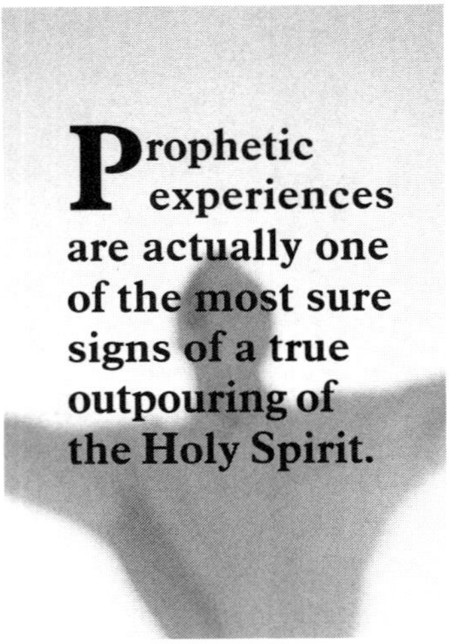

As the Apostle Paul later wrote to the Corinthians, he became more at home in the spiritual realm with the Lord than he was in his physical body. This is the nature of those who are maturing as a new creation. Just as Elisha could sit on the side of a hill in perfect peace, even though a whole army was about to attack him, he could see into the realm of the Spirit. We would not be overly concerned about any conditions on the earth if our spiritual eyes were truly open. If our spiritual eyes are open, we will see something even greater than Elijah, who saw myriads of angels protecting him—we will see Jesus who sits above all rule, authority, and dominion.

If we truly see Jesus and where He sits, and we know that we have been sent by Him, how could we fear anything or anyone on this earth? The Lord Jesus Himself walked this way, seeing what the Father was doing, and He gave us His Holy Spirit so that we can walk the same way. Being born again is just the beginning of our new creation lives, just as being born is the beginning of our lives in the natural realm. Our spiritual nature is something we must grow up into, which is in truth, growing up into Christ and becoming a functioning member of His body on the earth.

We cannot see the kingdom without being born again, but not all who are born again see the kingdom. Many who are born again refuse to see, for fear or other reasons, and they may mature some, but remain quite blind spiritually. This must change. The reason these prophetic experiences are being poured out by the Holy Spirit **"in the last days"** is because we are going to need this kind of guidance through the times ahead. We must have our eyes opened to see, and we must mature in our spiritual nature.

The way Jesus preached the kingdom was to demonstrate its authority over any conditions on the earth. Jesus Himself was God touching the earth with heaven. In heaven, there are no cripples, so when Jesus touched a cripple on the earth with heaven, he was healed. There is no lack in heaven, so when the great need of feeding over 5,000 hungry people with only one little boy's lunch arose, the Lord gave that little lunch a touch from heaven and it multiplied until all were fed and much was left over. In the times to come, when the last great trumpet of God is sounded, which is the preaching of the gospel of the kingdom, those who preach it will do so with the power to demonstrate the kingdom of heaven's authority over the earth and any conditions here that the Lord wants to touch with heaven.

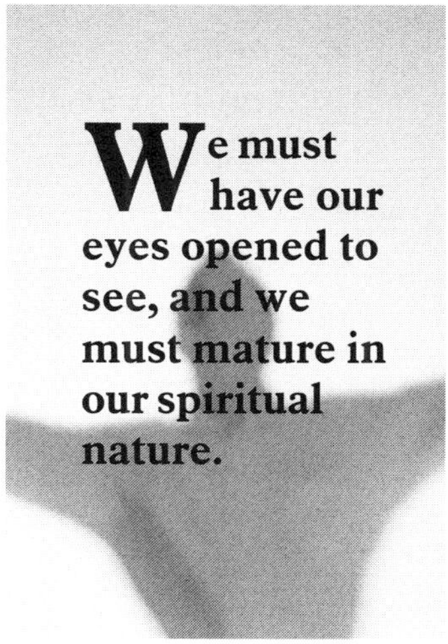

When Peter got out of the boat and walked on water, he was not literally walking on the water, he was walking on the Lord's Word by being obedient when He said **"Come" (see Matthew 14:29).** The Word of the Lord has more substance than the firmament. If the King of heaven says to a mountain to be plucked up and cast into the sea, and we are used by Him to do this, the whole world would be astonished, but the angels in heaven would probably be bored. They have seen much greater things than this—they have seen Him stretch out the heavens like a tent curtain.

We do not have terms in human language that can describe just how awesome our God is. It is His gentleness with us that allows His kingdom to be declared by "the foolishness of preaching" (see I Corinthians 1:21). When the Jews asked Jesus for a sign from heaven, they wanted Him to do something in the sky—stop the sun like He did for Joshua, or something of that nature which in no way could be done by a mere man. The Lord could have easily done this, but it was not the Father's time for that, so He did not. However, at the end of this age, we can expect much of that type of demonstration of heaven's authority over the earth, which is what the rest of the text in Acts 2 makes clear:

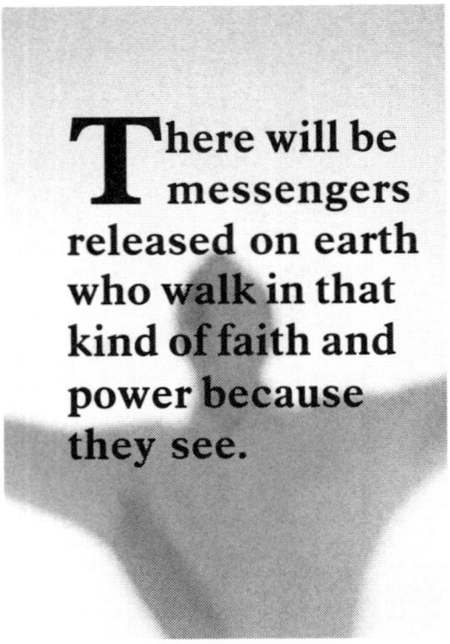

> **I will show wonders in heaven above and signs in the earth beneath: blood and fire and vapor of smoke.**
>
> **The sun shall be turned into darkness, and the moon into blood, before the coming of the great and awesome day of the Lord (Acts 2:19-20 NKJV).**

We are in the first stages of the time when the Lord will send messengers who will trump anything that even Hollywood has been able to imagine about men walking in supernatural power. I used to teach that many had moved mountains one shovelful at a time, but then I was chastised by the Lord in a dream for teaching that. He told me that those who had even a little faith could tell any mountain to be plucked up and cast into the sea, and it would obey them. He also said that this was going to be literally done before the end of this age as a witness that His Word is true.

There will be messengers released on earth who walk in that kind of faith and power because they see. They do not just see conditions as they are on the earth—they see the Lord and where He sits. They see what He wants to do, and they are used by Him to do it just as He was used by the Father to do His will.

My prayer for you is that you have faith to begin to see, to have the eyes of your heart opened, and to begin to live the kind of supernatural life you have been called to live. Some are entering now. Many others will follow, and by them, earth is about to be invaded again by heaven. If you are on this earth now, and know Jesus, this is your calling. It is who you really are. As one of the ancients said, "We are not called to be human beings who have occasional spiritual experiences, but we are spiritual beings who have occasional human experiences."

This is true, and it is exciting, but let us never forget that it is all about Jesus. He is the Ladder. The rungs on the Ladder that extend into heaven are the progressive revelation of who He is and where He is. That Ladder goes both ways, touching heaven and earth, because He loves man and He loves the earth, and will restore both mankind and the earth from all that was caused by the Fall. He is redeeming, reconciling, restoring, and above all He is love. We cannot truly mature in Him without growing in love for Him, and for all that He loves. ■

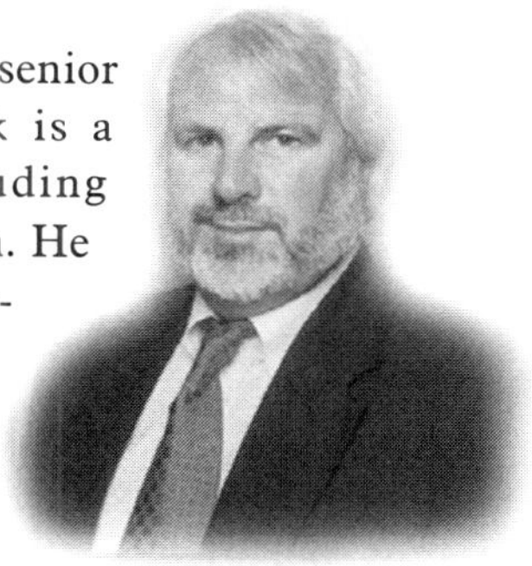

Rick Joyner is the founder, executive director, and senior pastor of MorningStar Fellowship Church. Rick is a well-known author of more than forty books, including his most recent, *The Harvest*, 20th Anniversary Edition. He also oversees MorningStar's School of Ministry, Fellowship of Ministries, and Fellowship of Churches. Rick and his wife, Julie, live in South Carolina and have five children: Anna, Aaryn, Amber, Ben, and Sam.

That which we persist in doing becomes easier—not that the nature of the task has changed, but our ability has increased.

—Ralph Waldo Emerson

Mustard Seeds of Wisdom

Spirit-Filled Ministry

by Larry Kreider

All Scripture references are New International Version unless otherwise noted.

What does the word "ministry" or "minister" really mean? *Webster's 1828 Dictionary* says, "to minister means to serve, to wait, or to attend." If you go to a restaurant, the waiter or waitress is ministering to you. They serve you or wait on you at your table. That is a type of ministry. If you go to a hospital, you will see hospital attendants who are waiting on, serving, or ministering to the patients. The terms "serve" and "minister" can be used interchangeably.

Every Christian is called by God to minister to other people. It is a privilege to minister and serve others in Jesus' name. There are many different ways to minister and many different types of ministry; however, each person is called to serve others in the name of Jesus. The Bible says in Mark 16:17-18 that some signs will accompany true disciples and confirm that the gospel message is genuine. **"And these signs will accompany those who believe: In my name they will drive out demons; they will speak in new tongues; they will pick up snakes with their hands; and when they drink deadly poison, it will not hurt them at all; they will place their hands on sick people, and they will get well."**

This Scripture speaks of various kinds of ministry to which the Lord calls His people today. It does not say that these signs shall follow pastors or apostles or evangelists. It says **"these signs will accompany those who believe."** Every Christian who truly believes in Jesus is called of God to be a minister to others and bring in the kingdom of God with power and authority.

When Jesus walked on the earth, He could be at only one place at one time. God the Father's strategy was for Jesus to go to the cross, then be raised from the dead, ascend into heaven, and later send the Holy Spirit to His people. The Holy Spirit then would indwell the Lord's people.

Now, rather than only Jesus walking the earth offering hope to people, there would be thousands of believers filled with the same Holy Spirit, ministering in Jesus' name throughout the world.

We have received the Holy Spirit and are called by the Lord to be ministers. Everywhere Jesus went, He ministered to people. Everywhere we go, God has called us to minister to others—in our homes, communities, schools, and jobs, and we can do it only by His strength. **"Not that we are competent in ourselves to claim anything for ourselves, but our competence comes from God. He has made us competent as ministers of a new covenant—not of the letter but of the Spirit; for the letter kills, but the Spirit gives life" (II Corinthians 3:5-6).**

I will never forget the first time I taught at a Bible study as a young man. I was scared because this was something new for me. I also realized that God's strength in me would pull me through. My competence was from God.

Let's Move Out of Our Comfort Zones

Each of us has an area in our lives that is comfortable, that we sometimes call our "comfort zone." We often find it hard to move out of our comfort zones into new things, but God has called us to take steps of faith. When Peter walked on the water, he moved far beyond his comfort zone!

God has called us to be people of faith and depend on the ability within us to help us accomplish His work. The Bible says: **"Without faith it is impossible to please God" (see Hebrews 11:6).** Ministry to others will often require us to move beyond our comfort zones.

Our homes are excellent places of ministry. Jesus spent much of His time in the homes of people. The Book of Acts is filled with examples of people meeting in homes: fellowshipping together, learning together, and ministering to one another. Invite people into your home—for a meal or to spend time in fellowship. Exciting things can happen when people sit down together to eat a meal, play a game, or just talk and laugh together. People can relax when we meet them on their own level and let them know we, too, are real people with real problems. We can ask the Lord for an opportunity to pray with them, and it can be a life-changing experience. Keep in mind that you are a saint who is called to minister.

The Lord may want to use you to give someone godly counsel. You may feel that since you are not a professional counselor, God cannot use you, but the Bible says in Isaiah 9:6: **"He will be called . . . Wonderful Counselor."** Jesus is the **"Counselor"** and He lives within us. When people need solutions to problems in their lives and I do not know the answers, I know that Jesus, the Counselor, lives in me. He has the answers. I pray and ask the Lord to speak to them and tell them what to do. Sometimes I can steer them toward other Christians who may be able to answer their questions.

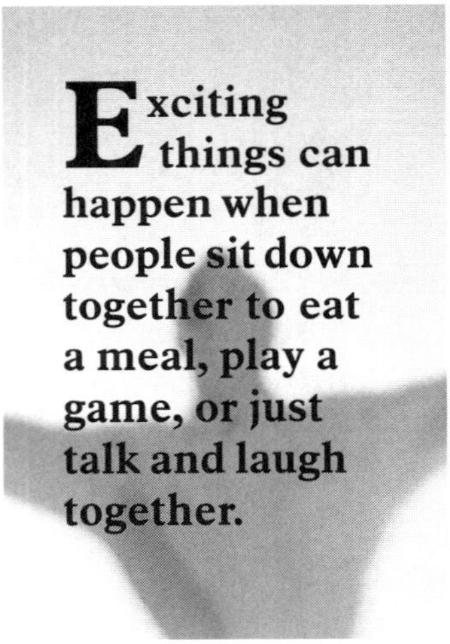

> **Exciting things can happen when people sit down together to eat a meal, play a game, or just talk and laugh together.**

Remember, the Lord has given you a powerful testimony! As you share your testimony with others, you'll find that the Holy Spirit will use you to speak the truth and others will be built up in faith. Perhaps you are afraid someone will ask you a question that you do not have the answer to. If you are unsure of the correct answers, it is appropriate to say, "I don't know, but perhaps I can ask someone who does know." None of us have all of the answers. That is why the Lord placed different gifts in different people in His church. We need one another.

God Has Chosen You to Minister

One of the greatest ways for us to experience and continue to build a love relationship with the Lord is to partner with Him. He desires to do His greater works through us. **"I tell you the truth, anyone who has**

faith in me will do what I have been doing. He will do even greater things than these, because I am going to the Father. And I will do whatever you ask in my name, so that the Son may bring glory to the Father. You may ask me for anything in my name, and I will do it" (John 14:12-14).

During the year that I was engaged to be married, we spent much of our time in ministry to young people. As we partnered together in ministry, the Lord allowed us to get to know one another better. This same concept is true in our relationship with our Lord Jesus. As we partner with Jesus and minister to others, we will continue to get to know Him more intimately.

Keep your "spiritual eyes" open. What is Jesus doing in your life, in the lives of your loved ones, or in the lives of those He has placed around you? How has He called you to partner with Him to minister and serve others? Expect the Lord to use you today, and remember **"...we have this treasure in jars of clay to show that this all-surpassing power is from God and not from us" (II Corinthians 4:7).**

We have the treasure, our Lord Jesus Christ, within us. The power we have to minister to others is not of us—it is from Him. We are weak **"jars of clay,"** but Jesus lives powerfully within our human weakness.

When you lay hands on sick people and pray, expect them to recover. Christ lives in you! As you speak words of encouragement to others, expect the Lord to use you to boost their faith. And never forget—God, the King of the whole universe, has chosen you as one of His choice ministers! ■

Larry Kreider serves as International Director of DOVE Christian Fellowship International (DCFI), a worldwide network of churches. During the past two decades, he has trained Christian leaders nationally and internationally. He has authored several books, including *Hearing God 30 Different Ways* and *The Cry for Spiritual Fathers and Mothers.* Visit www.dcfi.org for more information.

The Language of the Spirit

by Rick Joyner

If you were going to live in another country, you would have to learn the language in order to get along with the people who live there. To live in the kingdom of God that we have been made citizens of, we likewise need to know the language of the Spirit. It is a spiritual kingdom, with a spiritual language, just as we are told in I Corinthians 2:12-13:

> **Now we have received, not the spirit of the world, but the Spirit who is from God, that we might know the things freely given to us by God,**
>
> **which things we also speak, not in words taught by human wisdom, but in those taught by the Spirit, combining spiritual thoughts with spiritual words.**

If you moved to a foreign country, you would begin to feel more at home there if you began to understand the language; the same is true in the kingdom—when you begin to learn the language of the Spirit, you will begin to feel more at home in the spiritual realm.

The Language of Heaven

Dreams and visions are the language of the Spirit. This is why we see in Joel 2 and Acts 2 that when the Spirit is poured out, dreams, visions, and prophecy are the result. Also, the more mature you become, the more advanced your language should be. Because we think in words, the more words we know, the more advanced our thinking can become. Likewise, to think about a certain subject, such as physics, we need to understand some of the vocabulary of physics. The same is true in the kingdom. In the specific aspects of the kingdom, we need to develop our spiritual vocabulary.

We think in words (think about it). Spiritual words open us up to a whole new way of thinking that is beyond the natural realm. This is sometimes abused, especially by the immature or the pseudo spiritual, who, wanting to be considered spiritual, will often say such things as, “My spirit understands that,” which interpreted really means, “I don’t have a clue what you’re talking about!” There is a spiritual delusion which implies that if we understand something with our minds, then it cannot be spiritual, which is a very basic deception. If you do not understand something, then you do not understand it, period.

There is a joke that illustrates this point. It was in the time when the transplanting of organs had become so advanced that they were able to transplant brains. A man who was considering such a brain transplant was asking the doctor what his options were, and the doctor replied that he could buy the brain of a brilliant teacher for $5,000, a brilliant scientist for $10,000, or the brain of a Pentecostal or Charismatic for $50,000. When he asked why the brain of a Pentecostal or Charismatic was so expensive he was told, “That’s because it has not been used.”

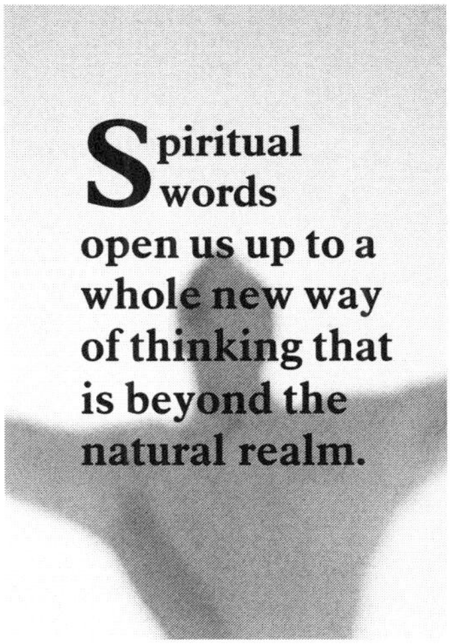

I am sure that is not funny to some, but there is a tragic truth to it, which is probably the result of a tragic misunderstanding of the next verses in this text in I Corinthians 2:

> **But a natural man does not accept the things of the Spirit of God; for they are foolishness to him, and he cannot understand them, because they are spiritually appraised.**
>
> **But he who is spiritual appraises all things, yet he himself is appraised by no man.**
>
> **For who has known the mind of the Lord, that he should instruct Him? But we have the mind of Christ (I Corinthians 2:14-16).**

The word **"natural"** here could have been translated "carnal," and speaks of one who sees and understands from the natural or carnal perspective. However, this does not mean that Christians, who are supposed to have "renewed minds," which are spiritually discerning minds, cannot understand spiritual things with their minds, but rather they should be able to appraise or understand **"all things,"** spiritual or natural, which is what this text of Scripture actually says.

Born-again, Spirit-filled Christians should have the greatest minds of all, able to understand clearly the things of the Spirit—with their minds. It is true that some things that we perceive and understand in the spiritual realm are hard to put into human words because our human language is limited. However, this does not mean that we cannot understand it—it just means we need a greater language for it. That greater language is the language of the Spirit, which we begin to understand through dreams and visions.

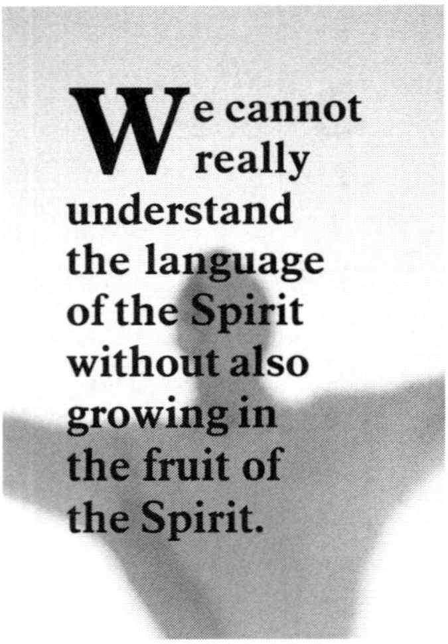
We cannot really understand the language of the Spirit without also growing in the fruit of the Spirit.

The first step to understanding the language of the Spirit is not to just try and understand symbolism, but to grasp that the language of the Spirit is a language of the heart and the mind together. When the Lord communicates prophetically what He is doing, He is conveying more than just the facts of coming events. He is also usually communicating why these events are taking place, especially if He is initiating them, because He wants His people to be one with Him in mind and heart. This is why we cannot really understand the language of the Spirit without also growing in the fruit of the Spirit.

Jon Amos Comenius, the great Moravian bishop who is considered the father of modern education, was the first to use illustrations in books because he said, "A picture is worth a thousand words." There is a great spiritual truth to this, which is why the Spirit uses dreams and visions to speak to us. If the Spirit was just trying to convey certain facts to us, it would be much easier for Him to just speak to us in plain English or whatever our native language is. When He speaks in dreams and visions, He is trying to communicate much more than just facts to us—He is communicating His heart as well. Therefore, we must also resolve to go beyond just getting the instructions from a dream or vision to getting the whole message.

Children like to play, and they like to play with words. This is why nursery rhymes are used to help them develop their communication skills. However, the older we get, the more mature and more serious our language and reading material becomes. As we get older, we go from nursery rhymes to novels, or even such things as technical manuals. Likewise, many of the dreams and visions given by the Spirit in times past have been on a more basic level, but as we mature we graduate to more advanced communications.

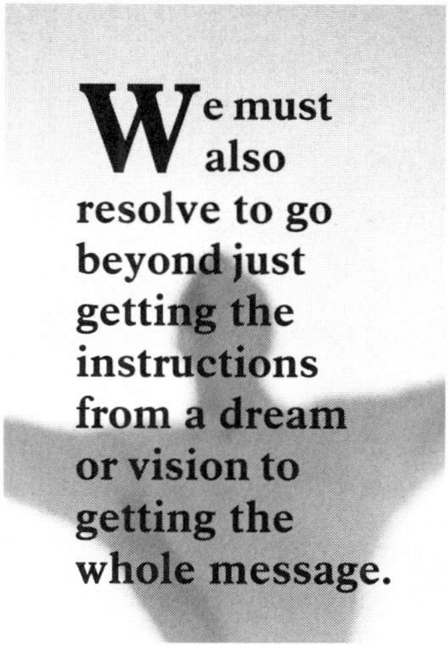

Entering "Mid-Heaven"

Many years ago, Steve Thompson started working with the prophetically-gifted people in our local congregation and formed them into "prophetic teams." Soon people were coming from all over the world just to receive ministry from these teams. They are remarkable, with real prophetic gifts. For years now, they have served at our Friday night and Sunday morning services, as well as at our conferences. Both Steve and I thought that these teams, mostly made up of prophetic novices, would make many mistakes, and we would of course hear a lot about these mistakes. To our great surprise, we started receiving literally thousands of positive reports about the accuracy and helpfulness of these teams, and very rarely a negative one. Many of these reports have been truly amazing in how accurately and clearly these teams were hearing from God. Some of these prophecies not only changed lives, but changed whole churches and movements.

Now we are having many people come back for a second time and we are receiving many reports about how these teams have matured, and those receiving ministry are even more astonished by how much more specific and clear these prophetic teams are now in their prophecies. It is true that they have matured and are now ministering on a much higher level than just a few years ago, but we are still on an elementary level in our prophetic ministry. However, many of our prophetic people are about to graduate from the elementary and be promoted to "middle school."

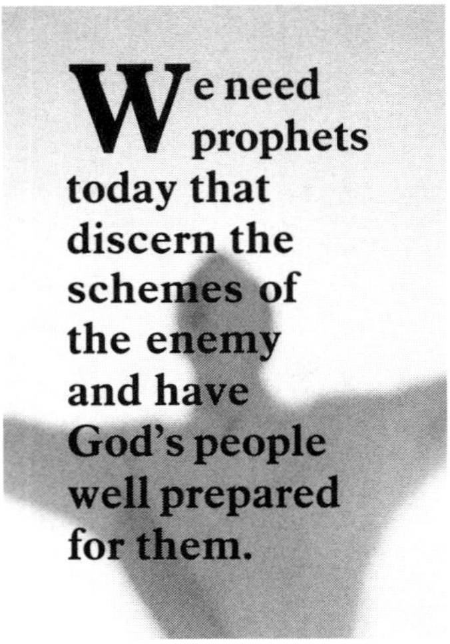

The elementary level of the prophetic that we have been enjoying is pretty good, and just as a community will have an elementary, middle, and high school, we need all three in our churches. We should never abandon the elementary just because some have moved on to higher levels, but we should continue to have a place where people can grow strong in the basics. However, there is a point when one needs to leave the elementary teachings and go on to the higher levels, and we need to make provision for this now.

Many look at the extraordinary prophets in the Old Testament as the highest standard of the prophetic, but before this age closes, there will be a prophetic ministry in the church that surpasses anything experienced under the Old Covenant. We have been given "a better covenant" with "a greater glory," and this will be demonstrated in all ways, including the level of prophetic ministry.

This is a high standard. There was a prophetic ministry in the Old Testament that knew everything that was said by enemies, even in the king's innermost chambers. Likewise, we need prophets today that discern the schemes of the enemy and have God's people well prepared for them. There were prophets in the Old Testament who were shocked when anything of significance happened that they did not foresee. Presently, we are instead shocked when we do foresee something accurately. This must change, and it is.

We do still have a long way to go just to get to the level of prophecy attained under the Old Covenant, but there will be New Covenant prophets who greatly exceed anything under the Old, even to the point of making the Jews jealous. This must be as a testimony of the glory of the New Covenant, but also because the times are going to require such a ministry. There are prophets being raised up now who will foresee every major event and will have God's people prepared for them.

The Watchmen

In the Old Testament, prophets were often called watchmen because they performed that duty for their cities, and some for the nation of Israel. Every church should have trustworthy watchmen on the walls who can spiritually see any enemy or friend coming from afar, and have good communication established with the elders who sit in the gates so that they can determine who to open the gates for or fortify them against. When the church has such a ministry, she will then be able to provide such a ministry to cities and even nations. Presently, there are very few churches that have a true watchman ministry in place.

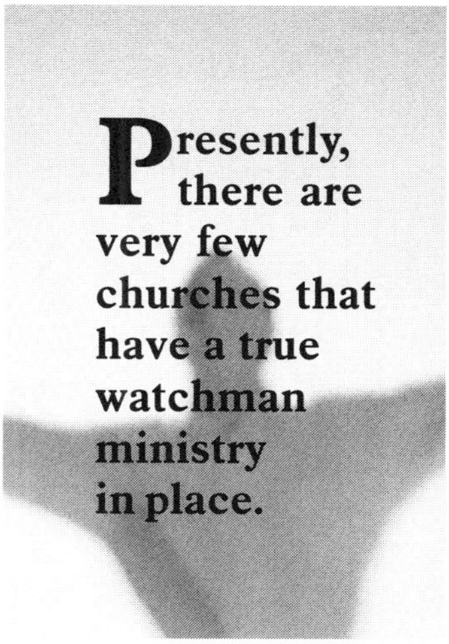

Just as a city without walls is easily broken into (see Proverbs 25:28), a city with walls that does not have watchmen will also be easily penetrated. Many of the attacks and tragedies that God's people are experiencing would not be happening if there was a trustworthy watchman ministry, and if we are true shepherds we will raise up that ministry for our people.

Presently, there does not seem to be more than a handful of churches in the world that have such a ministry in even the most elementary form, and we are paying a terrible price for this. Many leaders blame the watchmen for not being accurate and trustworthy enough, and the prophetically-gifted blame the elders for not listening to them or trusting them. Blaming each other is not helping, but there is a general demand put upon prophetic people to start at a mature level without giving them the training or allowing them the experience which is required to be trustworthy and gain maturity.

I have heard leaders compare prophetic ministry to doctors, saying they would not want a doctor to operate on them who was not 100 percent accurate, and they do not want prophetic people ministering who are not 100 percent accurate. If we carry this comparison forward, we might compare the cost of health care that is now reaching crisis proportions to such an attitude. Because one mistake can cost a doctor his malpractice insurance, they cannot ever admit a mistake or their practice can be over. Since they cannot learn from mistakes or write about them so others can learn about them, an increasing number of people needlessly suffer from such mistakes. Learning from mistakes is basic for maturity in every discipline, including prophetic ministry.

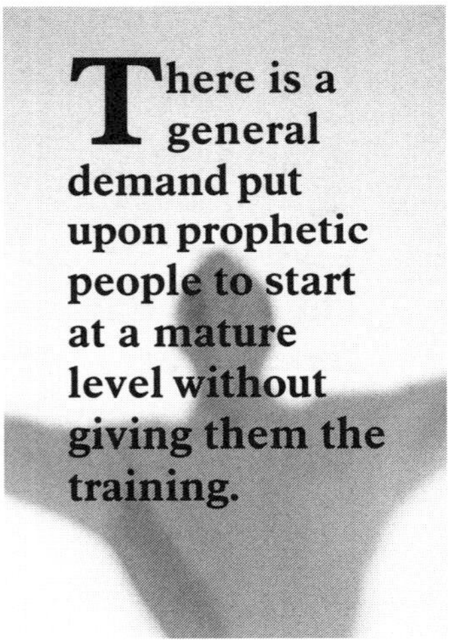

With doctors not being able to admit their mistakes for fear of lawsuits, it inhibits them from being able to give the most powerful medicine of all—hope. This is because if they are overly optimistic and things go worse than they had expected, they are in jeopardy. Therefore, they are almost always negative now, which really does not help the patients. Now this crisis is getting close to a meltdown in medicine, not only because many are now being discouraged from even entering the field by this scenario, but some of the most experienced and good doctors are leaving it. Mistakes must be faced and corrected, but not condemned or result in totally unrealistic punishment such as the lawsuits inflicted upon doctors today.

Likewise, these same kind of unrealistic repercussions for a mistake have discouraged many prophetic people from ever using their gifts, much less maturing in them. When we started our School of the Spirit meetings, the Lord instructed us to provide a place where His people could come, make mistakes, and not be condemned, but rather learn from them. We tried to honor the courage of those who stepped out to make mistakes. Those who are now walking in some of the most trustworthy ministries made some of the biggest and most humiliating mistakes in the beginning. However, God gives His grace to the humble, and those who embraced the humility and did not stop inevitably received more spiritual authority from the Lord.

Now, back to the metaphor of school. There needs to be standards attained before advancement. To pass those who do not meet the standards only devalues education in general. However, as Christianity is founded upon redemption, not condemnation, and helps those who have failed or made mistakes, we must develop a culture throughout the church that does not call failure success. Also it does not condemn failure, but rather redeems it and uses it to help those who make mistakes to learn from them, and therefore mature from them.

Why am I bringing all of this up in relation to the subject of the language of the Spirit? If you are going to learn another language, you must learn to accept the fact that you are not going to pronounce everything perfectly, that you are going to make some mistakes, and expect them to be comical, but you will learn faster and more this way. For the church to advance, or for any of us to advance spiritually, we must learn to recognize, accept, and use our mistakes. If you are afraid of that, you are almost certainly stuck right where you are.

Knowing the Subject

Fundamental to learning a foreign language is knowing the subject that a person is talking about. For example, if I am in a restaurant, and I know the waiter is talking about food, I can usually start to understand some of the words. If I am in a service and I know they are talking about the Lord, likewise I can start to pick out some words, and my vocabulary in that language will grow. My point here is that the most basic language of the Holy Spirit is Jesus. Second to this are redemption and restoration. Basically the entire Bible, except for the first two chapters and the last two, are about the essential subjects—redemption and restoration from the Fall.

Now to apply this, the ultimate purpose of the Holy Spirit is to bring forth Christ in His people. This is the foundation of true apostolic ministry as Paul declared it, to labor until Christ was formed in His people. This is why we are told in Revelation 19:10, **"For the testimony of Jesus is the spirit of prophecy."** Jesus is the Word—He is the communication of God.

We also know from John 17 that one of the most basic desires of the Lord for His people is unity. If we are going to really understand what is happening in the last days, we need to give far more attention to what Christ is doing than what the antichrist is doing. If we are in harmony with the Holy Spirit, He is looking at every situation to use it for redemption and restoration. There are some cases where separation is necessary, such as when a group falls into serious error or sin, but we should be hearing much more about bringing unity to the church than things that would bring separation. We should very severely judge any revelation that would bring separation or division between believers.

The Devil's Words

Most of the divisions in the church are the result of unhealed wounds. Not to be too graphic, but it is said that after a major battle, the noise of the flies swarming to the wounds can sound like a great wind. In prophetic dreams and visions, flies often represent lies, which is why Satan is called Beelzebub, the "lord of the flies;" He is the "father of lies." Whenever there is a battle in a church, he will swarm to it with his lies to infect the wounds so that they cannot heal. Therefore, whenever I have been wounded by a person or situation, I am not going to trust any dream, vision, or other revelation that would seem to agitate or infect this wound. If the Lord is going to speak into this situation, it is much more likely going to be something that brings healing and restoration. The devil's words can be spiritual too, but his are easily discerned from the Lord's simply by the standard of wisdom we are given in James 3:13-18:

> **Who among you is wise and understanding? Let him show by his good behavior his deeds in the gentleness of wisdom.**
>
> **But if you have bitter jealousy and selfish ambition in your heart, do not be arrogant and so lie against the truth.**
>
> **This wisdom is not that which comes down from above, but is earthly, natural, demonic.**
>
> **For where jealousy and selfish ambition exist, there is disorder and every evil thing.**
>
> **But the wisdom from above is first pure, then peaceable, gentle, reasonable, full of mercy and good fruits, unwavering, without hypocrisy.**
>
> **And the seed whose fruit is righteousness is sown in peace by those who make peace.**

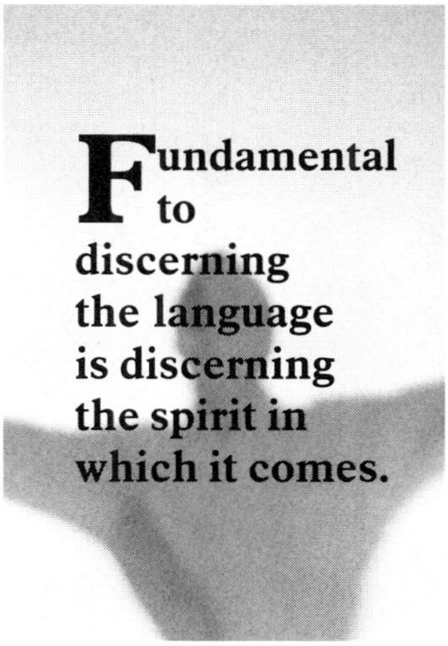

Fundamental to discerning the language is discerning the spirit in which it comes. Just previous to the verses quoted above, James refers to how difficult it is to tame the tongue, and how pure water and bitter water should not be coming out of the same source. How could the true condition of our spirits be discerned by our words?

This is why we must grow in the fruit of the Spirit to be trusted with greater revelation and authority. We will only be trusted with the higher ministry to the degree that we have strong foundations. Just as the great champions in sports, or the most successful people in every field, are those who do the fundamentals best, the same is true of the prophetic.

In Christianity, the fundamentals mostly relate to character issues—the more devoted we are to the fruit of the Spirit, the more we can be trusted with the power of the gifts of the Spirit. However, the fundamentals of the prophetic ministry are not entirely about character. There are matters such as discernment and interpretation, some of which can be learned through study, but most of which can only be learned by experience. Presently, there are not many safe churches for the young prophetic people to mature in, but we must provide them or we will pay an increasingly high price for it.

Because MorningStar has a reputation of being a place where those with prophetic gifts can come and develop, we have many coming from many places to be here, and we greatly appreciate having so many with such extraordinary gifts. We know we are only operating on the most basic, elementary level of prophetic ministry. There may be some who are much further along, and we hope so, but overall the church has not done very well in providing even elementary schools of the prophets. We must do this, and we must keep going higher. Just as in school, students who advance and do better at higher levels are those who mastered the language best at the previous level. The schools of the prophets must devote themselves to knowing much better the language of the Spirit. ■

To be a Christian without prayer is no more possible than to be alive without breathing.

—Martin Luther King, Jr.

Mustard Seeds of Wisdom

THE GREAT SOCIETY

The Power of New Testament Church Life

Domesticated Christianity

by Larry Ocasio

All Scripture references are New King James Version.

Recently, while watching a show on dog training, I was amazed at how the owners of a small beagle were completely confused at their pet's "odd" behavior. It seems that they could not keep him from sniffing, running, or hunting. The trainer, in absolute wonder responded, *"He's a beagle! That's what they do!"*

For the sake of having this dog's company, its owners are going to have to spend a lot of time, energy, and forethought to break the dog of the very reason for which it was created—hunting. With clever training methods, they will attempt to create an environment for this beagle that will be a substitute for his God-ordained purpose. This will enable them to receive whatever love and affection the dog will give them.

The picture is even more dramatic when we realize what we have done to birds. Think of this for a moment: Simply for the sake of having them as pets, we actually put birds in cages. These are creatures with wings! If that weren't enough of an oxymoron, in order to guard against the bird escaping, its wings are often clipped!

These are just two examples of our inclination to domesticate and tame the things we want in order to satisfy our desires. However, is it pets I'm troubled about? Certainly not—I myself am the owner of a cat and fully understand the blessing that pets can be. I am also fully aware of the need for organization and structure. Nevertheless, I believe that in the same way God used an ox to convey a financial truth, He is now using the domesticating of animals to reveal a disturbing trend that He is deeply concerned about.

> **"You shall not muzzle an ox while it treads out the grain."**
>
> **Is it oxen God is concerned about? Or does He say it altogether for our sakes? (see I Corinthians 9:9-10)**

In many ways, we have settled for a domesticated form of Christianity. Through religion, denominations, and self-preservation, we, too, have created an environment which keeps many of us in check, yet does little to fulfill our God-ordained purpose. Although this type of church-life has produced certain results, it still falls very short of the Christian experience the Bible says we can enjoy. Far too many believers currently sit bored out of their minds as the great works that the Lord says we can do are reduced to a list of all the things we *can't* do.

In many ways, we have settled for a domesticated form of Christianity.

Consequently, rather than pressing into the liberty and responsibility that comes along with living a Spirit-filled Christian life, many have settled for a "tamed" church experience which has *others* doing the hunting and flying as *we* sit in our "cages" week after week chewing on the "same old bone."

In our desire to make Christianity fit our needs, have we kept it from affecting our communities? Is our faith marked by how often we go to church, rather than by how often we "go about doing good"? Do we seek to get from weekly corporate gatherings what can only be obtained through daily intimate encounters with Jesus?

As leaders, have we domesticated Christianity so as to make people dependent upon *us* rather than upon the Lord? Have we cleverly devised programs and methods to keep people secure in our particular affiliation "cage"? How many "beagles" have we trained to quietly sit in our pews rather than equipping them to go out and hunt for the lost? Have we "clipped the wings" of God's people by teaching them more about what they *can't* do because they are Christians, than how high they *can* fly because they are Christians?

Martin Luther, Corrie ten Boom, Mother Theresa, Dr. Martin Luther King, Jr., and Ronald Reagan—these are but a few of the thousands of Christians that refused to be domesticated or satisfied by their "church attendance." Although these individuals fully understood the value of order, organization, and submission to authority, they were not willing to settle for anything less than all that God had for them. They are not alone. Today, believers all over the world are ministering to the hurting, saving the lost, and standing for truth against the moral decay of our day. They, too, are not content with simply sitting on a pew one day a week. They are daily out in the harvest fields "hunting" and "flying" as the Holy Spirit leads them.

From the very beginning, God intended for us to be co-laborers with Him. **"Then the LORD God took the man and put him in the garden of Eden to tend and keep it" (Genesis 2:15).** From cover to cover, the Bible is emphatic about man's participation *with* God in His activities on the earth. We were created for fellowship and to be yoked together *with* Christ as He fulfills His will *through* us.

From the very beginning, God intended for us to be co-laborers with Him.

> **Then He appointed twelve, that they might be with Him and that He might send them out to preach (Mark 3:14).**

These disciples were not relegated to a life of spectatorship as they sat at Jesus' feet and watched Him do all the work of ministry. In fact, it was quite the opposite. The entire purpose for their training was so that they could then do what Jesus Himself was doing, which is the essence and fruit of true Christianity.

> **These twelve Jesus sent out and commanded them, saying: "The kingdom of heaven is at hand.**

"Heal the sick, cleanse the lepers, raise the dead, cast out demons. Freely you have received, freely give" (see Matthew 10:5, 7-8).

Every congregation called by God should equip their saints for the work of the ministry (see Ephesians 4:12). There is not a single soul called into the kingdom that is without a God-given destiny. Our job as Christians is to find our place and help others to find theirs. As leaders, we have a responsibility to facilitate this exchange. If the people are not being equipped to fulfill their God-ordained purpose, then they are being domesticated to fulfill ours.

> **Our job as Christians is to find our place on the wall and help others to find theirs.**

The early church that Jesus left behind serves as a model for what ours should look like today. Contrary to popular opinion, Jesus did not merely have one hundred twenty members in His congregation when He concluded His earthly ministry. Numerically, there may have been one hundred twenty on that particular Pentecost Sunday, but how many who were part of His church were not there? And, what do you suppose they were doing?

Where do you suppose the woman at the well was during that time? What about the woman with the issue of blood, or the centurion whom Jesus proclaimed had a faith like none in Israel? Where was the wild man from the Gadarenes or the shepherds who showed up at His birth? What about the wise men who spent over two years looking for Him just to worship and give Him gifts? Do you imagine that all these individuals simply went home and kept their mouths shut?

There were many who followed Jesus who were not present at that meeting when the Holy Spirit descended; they were out telling others of the Messiah they had encountered. How do I know this? Because of the success the disciples had when they finally left the confines of Jerusalem with the gospel. Did we think that was merely a coincidence? Have we forgotten the principles of sowing, watering, and God giving the increase?

You and I are called to do great things with the Lord. We must not allow our faith to be domesticated by a particular day of the week or by focusing on all the stuff we cannot do. Of course, the Lord calls us to be part of a vibrant church and to steer clear of sin; however, that must never define our walk. Living for and with the Lord is what we were created to do. Going about doing good is in our DNA. Like the beagle hunts and the bird flies, Christians should go about doing the works of Christ.

> **Now when they saw the boldness of Peter and John, and perceived that they were uneducated and untrained men, they marveled. And they realized that they had been with Jesus (Acts 4:13).** ■

Larry Ocasio is the founder and president of Other Side Ministries, a preaching and writing ministry designed to "evangelize the saints" for the fulfillment of their destinies. Larry graduated from the MorningStar School of Ministry in Charlotte, North Carolina in 2000. He and his wife, Laurie, are currently living in Summerville, South Carolina. For more information you may visit his website at othersideministries.com or Larry can be contacted by email at: otherside@sc.rr.com

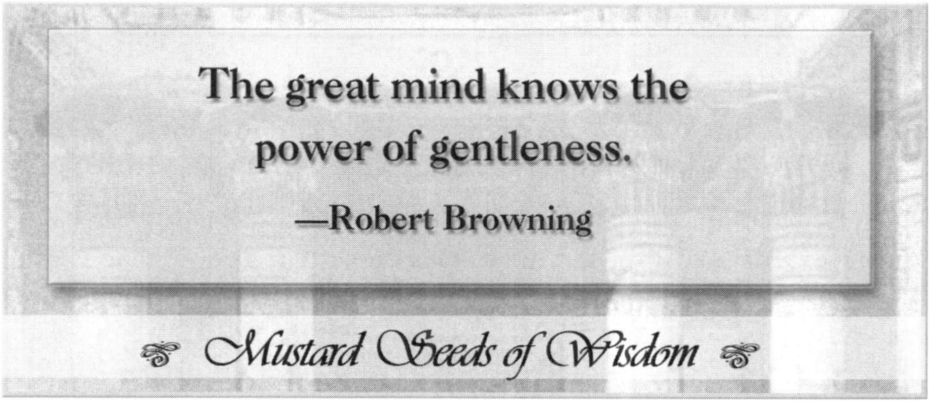

PROPHETIC PERSPECTIVES

Seeing Tomorrow Today, and How We Can Be Prepared For It

The Religious Spirit

by Bob Jones and Paul Keith Davis

While banished to the island of Patmos, the beloved disciple John was "in the Spirit" and was shown many great and mighty things through supernatural revelation. Jeremiah and Ezekiel both received revelations illustrated through symbols and imagery involving the people of their day. In the custom of these great prophets, our immutable Lord has continued to reveal spiritual truths characterized by various types and symbols through the spirit of prophecy. Very often, the revelations come in this manner to encourage us to seek the Lord for interpretation and application. Likewise, these revelations come in this pattern so that those with spiritual eyes and ears can understand them while confounding the natural mind. Spiritual truths can only be spiritually appraised as we depend upon the Holy Spirit for our counsel.

Many of the prophetic experiences given to Bob involve symbols and imagery of this nature. This is especially true with the one we are about to share which characterizes the religious spirit. It is not our attempt in this brief outline to exhaustively enumerate every attribute of the religious spirit, instead only those related to us in this revelation. Whenever spirits of this nature are identified, it is always beneficial to remind ourselves that we contend not against flesh and blood, only against principalities, powers, and spiritual wickedness in heavenly places (see Ephesians 6:12).

Our enemy does not consist of our fellow man, but of the evil influences released on the earth that operate through mankind setting themselves against the purposes of God. The great Apostle Paul entreats us to gently bring correction to those in opposition so perhaps God may grant repentance leading to the knowledge of the truth, that they may come to their senses and escape the snare of the devil, having been held captive by him to do his will (see II Timothy 2:25-26). That is our quest as well. The religious spirit is so closely akin to the Holy Spirit that the Lord announced it would deceive the very elect if possible.

The religious spirit is so closely akin to the Holy Spirit that the Lord announced it would deceive the very elect if possible.

THE ABOMINABLE SNOW-JOB MAN

In an allegorical prophetic experience, the religious spirit was illustrated to Bob with the appearance of the "abominable snowman," yet with the title of "Abominable Snow-Job Man." Each word in this description designates attributes of this spirit. The term "abominable snowman" first appeared in 1921 during a European expedition to Mount Everest led by Charles Kenneth Howard-Bury. After observing large footprints in the snow, Howard-Bury spotted distant figures through his binoculars. The explorer later told journalists that his Sherpa guides had called the creatures metoh-kangmi, a generic Nepalese term for mountain beasts. This word was accidentally mistranslated and suddenly news reports were claiming that explorers had seen a man-monster the natives called "the abominable snowman."

The vision portrayed this spirit in this design to illustrate its abominable quality from the Lord's perspective. To the natural eye, the religious spirit attempts to operate so close to the manner of the Holy

Spirit that it would be unrecognizable unless spiritually discerned. Thankfully, the Lord is communicating to us distinguishable attributes of this destructive enemy of our souls and the fruit that it bears.

In the vision, Bob was told that this spirit can be found in Isaiah 66:16-18 attempting to lead the people into the Divine Presence by an unlawful means resulting in the judgment of God.

> **For with fire and with his sword the LORD will execute judgment upon all men, and many will be those slain by the LORD.**
>
> **"Those who consecrate and purify themselves to go into the gardens, following the one in the midst of those who eat the flesh of pigs and rats and other abominable things—they will meet their end together," declares the LORD.**
>
> **"And I, because of their actions and their imaginations, am about to come and gather all nations and tongues, and they will come and see my glory" (NIV).**

It is an abomination to attempt to attain access to the Garden of the Lord in any other manner than the one prescribed by Him.

THE ABOMINATION

In Scripture, gardens derive their spiritual significance from the Garden of Eden, denoting a place of worship and intimate fellowship. During seasons of apostasy, gardens were utilized for idolatrous sacrifice. It is an abomination to attempt to attain access to the Garden of the Lord in any other manner than the one prescribed by Him. The religious spirit directs the people to sanctify themselves, but only in their minds, ministering to them the "flesh of swine" and "mice." These two biblically unclean animals represent unsanctified nourishment presented to the people through the soul of man rather than the Holy Spirit. These could depict intellectual comprehension and opinions of the Scriptures apart from the divine revelation released through the Spirit of Truth. This is abominable in the sight of the Lord.

Unsanctified thoughts and vain imaginations surrender opportunities to the enemy to loose anointed curses through this type of administration resulting in persecution and intimidation. The church becomes desolate when this spirit controls and feeds the temple of man. The abomination of desolation described in Daniel 11:31 and Matthew 24:15 foretell the operation of this spirit sustaining the people from the Tree of Knowledge of Good and Evil. We are the temple of God and must be sanctified in truth. The Lord described it as vain worship to honor Him with our lips, while removing our hearts far from Him by teaching for doctrine the precepts of men (see Matthew 15:8-9).

The religious spirit introduces the spirit of the world into the church nullifying the grace of God.

The Scriptures declare that the kingdom of God does not merely consist in words but also in power (see I Corinthians 4:20). Conversely, the "Abominable Snow-Job Man" is earthly, sensual, and unclean with an unsanctified temple displaying no Holy Spirit power. The power of this man pollutes our reasoning and explains away the sanctified temple of God and the power of the Holy Spirit through philosophical reasoning. This type of leadership will steal the spiritual seed in our hearts imparted through the true knowledge of Christ. The destination of those deceived by this spiritual reasoning is the pit of despair and fear. Satan then relishes the opportunity to capture these as he chooses to do his will, opposing the true anointing of Christ. This is made possible when the canopy of God's covering is breached through spiritual error advanced by this spirit.

The religious spirit introduces the spirit of the world into the church, nullifying the grace of God. The views of truth necessary to purify the church are not such as the world gives, but such as are communicated by the Spirit of God. This spirit will attempt to lead the church away from the reality of God expressed in the Book of Acts. During the latter years of his life, John G. Lake received a powerful angelic visitation. In this encounter, the angel opened the Scriptures to the Book of Acts saying, "This is Pentecost as God gave it through the heart of Jesus. Strive for this; contend for this . . . teach the people to pray for this. For this and this alone will meet the necessity of the human heart, and this alone will have power to overcome the forces of darkness." As the angel departed he admonished Brother Lake insisting, "Pray, pray, pray . . . Teach the people to pray. Prayer and prayer alone, much prayer, persistent prayer is the door of entrance to the heart of God."

Prayer and prayer alone, much prayer, persistent prayer is the door of entrance to the heart of God.

God's Reserves

In the vision, Bob saw what initially seemed to be an angel with female appearances descending from heaven. As the image advanced closer, he saw a name written upon her: EKKLESIA– "Called Out Ones." Close observation revealed that she had neither hands nor feet. This expressed that the proper biblical priesthood had not yet been released to the body to prepare her for unimpaired bridal duties. The Lord indicated that He was going to release the "Zadok" priesthood to teach the distinction between the clean and the profane (see Ezekiel 44:15-16). This ministry will be the government of God providing a cleansing light, purifying her to emerge as the glorious bride of Christ.

The Spirit then declared that He is calling forth His "reserves" to active duty. These reserves can be found in Jeremiah 50:20:

> **In those days, and in that time, saith the LORD, the iniquity of Israel shall be sought for, and there shall be none;**

and the sins of Judah, and they shall not be found: for I will pardon them whom I reserve (KJV).

The Lord is going to equip these "pardoned ones" with the authority of the "rod of iron" to serve as a bridge over troubled waters. The Holy Spirit will function as a bridge of deliverance leading to Calvary's cross. Reserves are defined as a military force withheld for use by a commander when he desires to commit those troops decisively to battle and enemy engagement. These will also be anointed with the Lord's "battle-axe" for the purpose of laying the axe to the root of the religious tree.

The Lord's desire is to bring a priesthood to the headship of His people that will feed the flock the pure revelation of Jesus Christ. The Word of God is seed and the Holy Spirit waters that seed to produce a divine, fruit-bearing tree. Wisdom comes from heaven down; human knowledge comes from the earth up. This distinction must be recognized in the church in preparation for the end-time harvest.

The Holy Spirit will function as a bridge of deliverance leading to Calvary's cross.

The Snow-Job

The Apostle Paul identified the religious spirit in II Corinthians 11:12-15.

But what I am doing, I will continue to do, that I may cut off opportunity from those who desire an opportunity to be regarded just as we are in the matter about which they are boasting.

For such men are false apostles, deceitful workers, disguising themselves as apostles of Christ.

And no wonder, for even Satan disguises himself as an angel of light.

Therefore it is not surprising if his servants also disguise themselves as servants of righteousness; whose end shall be according to their deeds.

The primary purpose of this spirit is to veil the minds of those without faith that the light of THE GOSPEL OF THE GLORY OF CHRIST, who is the image of the invisible God, should not shine unto them (see II Corinthians 4:4). This type of leadership will preach the sufferings of Christ, but not the glory. They will preach Christ crucified, but not Christ risen and the power of His resurrection. They will even preach the gospel of the grace of God but not the gospel of the GLORY OF CHRIST. It is the preaching of the glory of Christ which produces the greatest enmity from Satan and what he has worked so diligently to keep veiled from the eyes of the church.

> **The religious spirit attempts to direct a person to the favor of God through works and efforts of the flesh.**

The very essence of the "Abominable Snow-Job Man" is deception. It is a deception to preach the perfection that is attained on the actions and deeds of works, while our minds remain veiled to the redemption which is already ours in Christ Jesus. Out of necessity, the message of "deceitful ministers" must appear to be right and true or the message would not be deceiving. Simply having a zeal for God is not sufficient. It must be zeal accompanied with divine truth according to Romans 10:2-3. Even sincerity alone is not sufficient. Uzzah, from the sincerity of his heart, reached his hand to steady the ark of the Lord, yet it cost him his life because it did not follow the Lord's prescribed way.

It is from the heart that man BELIEVES which results in righteousness. Residing in a justified state results when the illumination of the heart grasps the pardoning grace of Christ, which introduces him to the favor of God. Even so, **"faith without works is dead" (see James 2:26),** but only as an outward expression of an inward conviction. The religious spirit attempts to direct a person to the favor of God through works and efforts of the flesh. Cain attempted to gain favor with God by offering the fruit of his labor and was rejected. Abel by revelation recognized his inability to adequately atone for his sin, offered the life of the innocent, and found favor with God.

Clearly, an internal distinction existed in the intention or disposition of these two sacrifices. Abel's sacrifice was offered through revelation and obedient faith with a sense of gratitude for mercy, followed by obedience to His will. Cain's offering, although requiring greater hardship and effort, was devoid of faith and rejected. This early Genesis account contrasted the heart of the religious spirit and the liberty obtained through obedience. **"Abraham believed God and it was reckoned to him as righteousness and he was called the friend of God" (see James 2:23).**

It is the gospel of the glory of Christ that is the greatest threat to the kingdom of darkness and it is this very gospel that must be demonstrated during this generation to bring the bride to the point of perfection. **"For God, who said, 'Light shall shine out of darkness,' is the One who has shone in our hearts to give the light of the KNOWLEDGE OF THE GLORY OF GOD IN THE FACE OF CHRIST" (II Corinthians 4:6).** ■

Bob Jones is a contemporary prophet with a great love for the Lord Jesus and His truth. His prophesies have spanned over three decades as the Lord has enabled him to foretell earthquakes, tidal waves, comets, and weather patterns. Like Daniel who functioned at an incredible level, Bob has often told leaders their dreams and experiences, as well as the interpretation. After years of running from God, Bob came to a wonderful salvation more than thirty years ago. He has moved with a clear revelatory gifting, accompanied by gifts of healing and miracles since that time.

Paul Keith Davis and his wife, Wanda, are the founders of WhiteDove Ministries. They travel extensively, imparting the end-time mandate of preparation for the glory and manifest presence of Christ. He and Bob Jones write *The Shepherd's Rod* yearly. Paul Keith has also written the book, *The Thrones of Our Soul.* He and his wife reside in Alabama. Together they have five children and three grandchildren.

The Holy Spirit and the Arts

by Rick Joyner and Amanda Prychodko

In the Bible, artists were the first people to be filled with the Holy Spirit. In the Old Testament, we often find quotes saying that the Spirit of God came on someone, such as we see in II Chronicles 15:1, **"Now the Spirit of God came on Azariah the son of Oded,"** or in II Chronicles 24:20, **"Then the Spirit of God came on Zechariah the son of Jehoiada the priest...."** However, it was Bezalel who was the first person in the Bible about whom it was said that he was "filled with the Spirit," which we see in Exodus 31:1-5:

> **Now the LORD spoke to Moses, saying,**
>
> **"See, I have called by name Bezalel, the son of Uri, the son of Hur, of the tribe of Judah.**
>
> **"And I have *filled* him with the Spirit of God in wisdom, in understanding, in knowledge, and in all kinds of craftsmanship,**
>
> **to make artistic designs for work in gold, in silver, and in bronze,**
>
> **and in the cutting of stones for settings, and in the carving of wood, that he may work in all kinds of craftsmanship."**

Bezalel means "under the shadow, protection of God." Isn't it interesting that the first person in the Bible who was said to be "filled with the Spirit" was an artisan, and not a priest, king, or prophet? This should give us a definite sense of the importance that the Lord gave for art in His dwelling place, the tabernacle. If there was ever a building that exceeded this one for artistic excellence, it would have to be His other dwelling place in the Old Testament, the temple that Solomon built for Him. This should declare to us the importance that He gives to art in His church, His present dwelling place.

The significance of art in the church is an important prophetic truth for our time. The Lord gave the vision of what His tabernacle was to be like to Moses, but He did not give the wisdom for practical work for building His dwelling place to an architect, an engineer, or a priest—He gave it to an artist. There is an important message in this for those whose hearts burn to see the Lord have a place to dwell among His people.

ARTISTS CLOTHED THE PRIESTS

In Exodus 28:3, we see that the artists working with Bezalel were also filled with the Holy Spirit, **"So you shall speak to all who are gifted artisans, whom I have filled with the spirit of wisdom, that they may make Aaron's garments, to consecrate him, that he may minister to Me as priest" (NKJV).** Here we also see that the Lord wanted artists to make the priests' garments. How would this apply to us? It seems that there is a special revelation of the Lord which can come through art that touches His basic nature as the Creator. This is why those who know Him, and are changed into His image by seeing Him, should also be creative. Creativity is His basic nature. Therefore, Christians should be the most creative people on the earth, and art that is inspired by the Holy Spirit should be worn by the priests of the Lord like a garment.

Christians should be the most creative people on the earth.

We should also consider that artists, who are inspired by the Holy Spirit, and who will earnestly follow Him as Bezalel did, do have a similar role like prophets and priests to reveal Him to the people. To reveal the Lord is in fact the most basic purpose of art, and not only is it the highest form of art, it is the only true fulfillment that an artist will ever have. Anything else will only lead to a base reduction or perversion of the gift.

Throughout much of the church age, the church was the great custodian of art, and most of the great works of art were commissioned by the church. As the church at times drifted from her pure devotion to the Lord, the art commissioned by the church also drifted. When the Protestant Reformation began, there was a great reaction to much of the church's art that was believed to be used as idolatry, so many of the

Protestant movements rejected art altogether in worship. This led to the building of very plain and colorless buildings for the church's meeting places, which was also a good reflection of the church services, and therefore became a reflection of the way that many perceived God.

This is one of the great tragedies of church history and has misrepresented God possibly as much as that which was considered idolatry. God is the most wonderful, interesting, colorful, and creative One there is, or will ever be. Just look at His creation! His people should reflect this.

There is a movement in the church today to recover art in worship, and it is not unexpected that it is taking place chiefly among those baptized in the Holy Spirit or those who at least seek to be "Spirit-filled." Those who are truly filled with His Spirit will not be able to contain the creativity that is a basic nature of the Spirit for very long.

> **God is the most wonderful, interesting, colorful, and creative One there is, or will ever be.**

However, it is crucial that artists are deeply committed to worshiping the Lord with their art, and not worshiping art itself or artists. There are ditches on either side of the path of life—lawlessness on one side and legalism on the other. In art, this is usually manifested in idolatry on one side, which is a form of lawlessness, and an inhibiting legalism on the other side. Learning to navigate between these extremes is often difficult, but the tension between them can help keep us in the proper balance with where the path of life is, keeping life in our art.

Clothed With His Glory

It is noteworthy that the Hebrew verb *mashach*, which means "to anoint" is defined as, "to smear with oil, or paint" (Strong's OT: 4886). There is a filling of the Spirit, and an anointing or painting of the Spirit. We should have the nature of the Spirit in our hearts, and this should be reflected on us too. We know the meanings of this in relation to ministry and the anointing we must have for ministry, but think about it in relation to art: how we are clothed. This was a high purpose for art in the Old Testament—to clothe the priests.

We know from the parable of the wedding feast in Matthew 22 that the Lord Himself will be offended if we are not properly attired for the occasion. To dress properly for a wedding is a basic way that we show respect for the bride and groom and their families. The same would be true for a funeral or other occasions such as meeting with a dignitary, leader, or boss. To be careless with how we dress for an occasion is to show that we "care less" about it.

Now think about those who dress just to attract attention to themselves. Such are obvious, and though they may have dressed attractively, self-centeredness is never really attractive except in a carnal way. True respect for such people is not going to be built in this way. However, if a person dresses well, thinking about the person or people they are going to see, there is a different sense from them—a certain dignity and respect that is not self-centered and will inevitably command respect.

We need to likewise treat our art this way—seeking to make it an honor to the One we are doing it for, not to just draw attention to ourselves or our art. There will always be certain crudeness with the art of an artist who is self-seeking and self-promoting, which will show through any amount of talent. Likewise, the art of those who have a higher purpose for their art than seeking to be known or seen themselves will also stand out. There will be a dignity and class to this art, a true nobility of spirit that is holy, which will show through the art.

The Holy Spirit's first name is "Holy," and if we truly have and follow the Spirit, we will be holy and our work will be too. In I Chronicles 16:29, II Chronicles 20:21, Psalm 29:2, and Psalm 96:9 (KJV), there is a "**beauty of holiness.**" The beauty of holiness will eclipse any earthly beauty like the sun and the moon when they rise. The moon is beautiful, but it only

The beauty of holiness will eclipse any earthly beauty like the sun and the moon when they rise.

reflects the sun's light and will fade quickly when the sun itself rises. There is a beauty of holiness coming that will eclipse all other beauty on the earth. Prophetic artists will see it and prophesy it, but this can only be done from a holy life. Anything less will cloud and obscure the vision of this beauty.

It has been said by the experts that the future of art is perversion. That is the devil's prophecy. The Lord has another opinion. Remember how communists said for seventy years that God was not real, and in one day the Lord said communism was not real and it fell apart? The same will always happen to the counterfeit when the real appears. Real creativity is coming to the arts, and it will come through a pure and holy movement which esteems truth and true beauty.

There is a beauty of holiness coming that will eclipse all other beauty on the earth.

If God has called us to something, there will obviously be talent, and we want to do all that we do with excellence, but excellence of character is the foundation of excellence in our work. **"Out of the abundance of the heart the mouth speaks" (see Matthew 12:34 NKJV),** and out of the abundance of the heart the artist creates. What is coming from the Lord will be pure and holy, and without bitterness or rebellion. It will be pure worship of the One who is worthy. No light has been seen in art like this before, and it will take the world of art by storm. When the church takes back what is rightfully hers, the Son rising in art will be like the rising sun that burns away the fog. This fog was the result of the church being abandoned to the world, where it has drifted without direction or purpose. Direction and purpose are going to be recovered when they are recovered by the church.

Art Prophesies

We also see in both Joel 2 and Acts 2 that when the Spirit is poured out there will be prophecy. Art has in fact been a primary media for prophecy, both for good and evil. By its very nature, art usually predicts and points ahead to trends that cultures follow. Art also becomes a primary media for interpreting the trends. It is for this reason that the church should be especially devoted to the arts as it is called to be the light of the world, pointing the way and illuminating the path. When the church truly follows the Spirit and becomes what she is called to be in our time, we can expect prophetic Christians to begin to lead in every field of art.

Some artists will be called to bring the church to a higher level of the prophetic. After God gave the Holy Spirit to Bezalel to fill him with special ability, wisdom, and craftsmanship, we do not see Him doing this in Scripture to that extent again. However, we have "a better covenant" and should expect something even greater through Christ. We should expect better prophets under the New Covenant than there were under the Old Covenant, and we should expect a greater anointing on prophetic art as well.

We can expect some artists to create paintings that will come straight from the throne room of God.

We can expect some artists to create paintings that will come straight from the throne room of God. By looking at them, people in the church will get impartations of colors, a deeper prophetic vision, and heavenly understanding. They will get an impartation of the same anointing. In the same way, people with other creative gifts such as music or writing will receive this greater anointing, and through them the whole church will be drawn to the throne from which it came.

God, through Moses, gave Bezalel instructions on how to build His habitation. Bezalel knew clearly what colors to use and where to use them. He got architectural plans and was instructed on how to create the lampstand, the altar, the laver, and all of the other furniture and coverings to be placed there. He was instructed on how to weave colors and images into the tent walls and curtains and how to create holy garments for the priests. Until the tent was built, only Moses, Bezalel, and the artists working with Bezalel could see it in their spirits. But once the tent was built, everyone could see it, but not everyone could see it to the same extent. The deeper they were allowed to enter the temple, the more they could see. Today, we all have access to the deepest part of the temple.

Just as Bezalel saw the tent first and then, once it was built, all could see it, so will some artists in the church see things first. Then they will express them and people seeing those images will see deeper in the Spirit because of the anointing that the Holy Spirit is pouring out through the arts. All art and creativity are given to draw us closer to the Artist, the Creator.

Build the Highway

The Lord obviously wants to share His creativity with His people. It is the basic nature of the New Covenant that we do not have to be perfect to come into the Lord's presence, but we get perfected by coming into His presence. The closer we are to Him, the more clean and pure we shall be—our art will reflect this. Those who have seen His glory will not be very impressed by the greatest human glory. Those who have seen His creativity will not be very impressed by the greatest human creativity.

The closer we are to Him, the more clean and pure we shall be— our art will reflect this.

For this reason, the closer we get to Him the less our art should be influenced by human art or human trends, but should reflect heavenly trends that will often be in direct contrast to the nature of fallen human creativity. One of the saddest statements of the present condition of the church is when it follows the world's trends in art and music. The world should be following the church, and the closer we get to God, the more we can be sure that art and music will be clean and pure.

The Lord is seeking clean vessels to release His creativity. Many artists in the church are in bondage because they have very worldly ideas and desires, similar to artists in the world—namely, wrong ideas of success, selfish ambitions, jealousy, and pride. Art and artists have always been under a lot of attack by the enemy because the enemy knows what a powerful vessel they can be for good or evil. Many artists are outcasts, rejected and poor, but then others are exalted to be like gods. Yet the Lord promises that He will bring low those who exalt themselves, and will exalt those who humble themselves. All exaltation by men is brief, shallow, and terribly empty. This is why almost everyone who reaches a pinnacle in a field of art or almost anything else falls into a deep depression.

When we attain pinnacles out of selfish ambition, it is never what is expected, but much, much less. When the Lord takes us to the heights, it is different. We begin to breathe the atmosphere of heaven and glories beyond human imagination begin to be discerned in their nature of being ever-expanding and ever-increasing, just like the universe He created. One aspect of heaven is a continual marvel and wonder at what God has done, and the unfathomable privilege of being able to participate with Him in some of it. Compared to God, even the greatest human genius or art form will be like a molecule standing before the sun; but the fact that the sun cares about, and even loves that little molecule, causes an ever-increasing love of the little molecule for the sun.

The Lord promises that He will bring low those who exalt themselves, and will exalt those who humble themselves.

Artistic expression is an expression of creativity. Creativity is spiritual and therefore has a power and influence that can be greater than is apparent. Because of this, the enemy tries to influence artists and use them for his purpose. Art has been used for much evil, but it will be redeemed and fully restored like all of the gifts that the Lord gave to man so that man could better relate to Him. As the Lord Jesus states in Luke 3:4-5, which He quoted from the Prophet Isaiah:

"The voice of one crying in the wilderness, 'Make ready the way of the Lord, make His paths straight.

'Every ravine will be filled, and every mountain and hill will be brought low; the crooked will become straight, and the rough roads smooth.'"

We are again in the time of Elijah, preparing the way for the coming of the Lord. This is how we are building the highway on which He will come—we will level the mountains, bring up the low places, and make the crooked paths straight. The mountains here are strongholds, and the low places are the oppressed. In relation to the arts, the crooked paths are the self-worship, humanism, and perversions which have taken over the arts. Some are now arising with divinely powerful weapons to bring down the strongholds and tools for building the highway. These will see the glory of the Lord come down with what they have been used to build. It will be worth the struggle. It is a noble cause, the "good fight" of faith—it will take much faith, but the victory is sure for those who remain faithful. Don't ever give up. ■

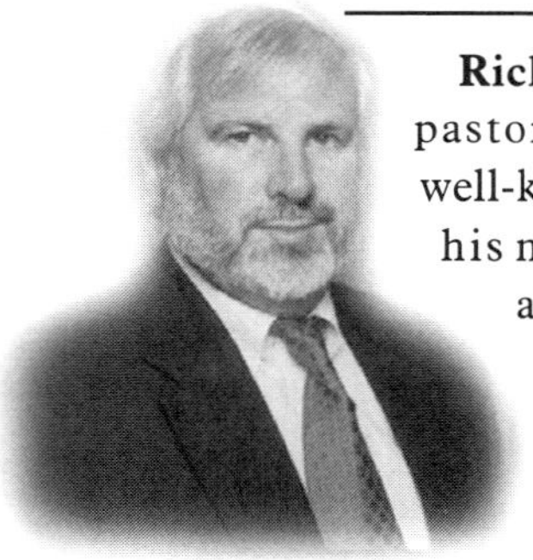

Rick Joyner is the founder, executive director, and senior pastor of MorningStar Fellowship Church. Rick is a well-known author of more than forty books, including his most recent, *The Harvest*, 20th Anniversary Edition. He also oversees MorningStar's School of Ministry, Fellowship of Ministries, and Fellowship of Churches. Rick and his wife, Julie, live in South Carolina and have five children: Anna, Aaryn, Amber, Ben, and Sam.

Amanda Prychodko studied at the Academy of Fine Arts in Vienna, Austria and has worked mostly in Paris and Switzerland. She has exhibited internationally, notably with two historical art galleries. Along with her husband, Andrei, she teaches and heads fine art at MorningStar Ministries at H.I.M. She has held creativity workshops in the United States and Europe. Her vision is to see art flourishing again in the church.

A Christian Approach to the Environment

by Anna Jane Joyner

All Scripture references are New International Version unless otherwise noted.

Introduction by Rick Joyner

The following is a thesis that my daughter, Anna, wrote for a course while studying at the University of North Carolina. Even though this was written for a secular audience, it contains important facts that Christians need to consider, which explain some basic insights about both Christian movements and the resulting impact they have had on some doctrines concerning attitudes toward the environment. Like it or not, agree with it or not, this is becoming one of the crucial and defining issues of our time and Christians should be leading the way, shining the light on these issues, not avoiding them. This is why we are including this under the section, "Prophetic Perspectives."

Please also note that it is "a" Christian approach, not "the." This is an issue bigger than can be contained in a single article. Though I think Anna did a remarkable job stating the essence of some of the Christian movements that were covered in her thesis, no doubt many from those movements will object that there is far more to their doctrine than is presented here. This is understood as the only areas covered are those which affected people's perspective of the environment, and certainly many within each of these movements may have a very different perspective on these issues. However, in a general sense the insights are valid, and in some cases should be cause for reconsideration, not just to protect the creation, but to obey the Creator.

The basic Christian responsibility to be a light to the world means having answers to the world's most pressing issues and leading the way to finding solutions to them. We know from Scripture that the Lord cares so much about His creation that He knows when a single sparrow falls to the ground. The greatest gift that God has given to man is His Son, and then of course His Holy Spirit. However, this creation is a wonderful gift, and to appreciate any gift is to also appreciate the Giver. I know that if I gave someone a gift, and they abused it or neglected it, I probably would not give them anything else of value and would take it as a personal affront. This is likewise such an affront to God that in Revelation 11:18 He declares that He will ***"...destroy those who destroy the earth."***

In discussing this issue with Christians, I usually receive the response that many who devote themselves to environmental issues go to extremes, even loving the creation and worshiping it more than the Creator, and this is true. However, is it not likely that such extremes exist because Christians, who are supposed to be the light of the world, are not addressing these issues with sound wisdom and balance?

Global warming is becoming one of the foremost and most controversial issues of our time. There are extremes on both sides. Liberals see conservatives as protectors of the greedy who are the most responsible for the problems, and conservatives see liberals as constantly inventing a crisis so they can pretend to save the world and are even more prone to use fear and pressure tactics than the right-wing extremists they continually vilify. There is truth to both of these positions. There are also noteworthy scientists taking both sides concerning the cause of global warming, though there are few who are denying that it is in fact happening. Even so, regardless of the issue of global warming, Christians should be the most diligent and faithful protectors of the environment. We should be doing many of the things that those who are so focused on global warming propose, even if there was no global warming.

Global warming is becoming one of the foremost and most controversial issues of our time.

There is presently a case made for not going to the extremes which some are calling for; however, the longer we wait to take more moderate measures, the more likely we will in fact have to take extreme measures, and there is also the very real danger that if we delay too long, even the extreme measures will no longer save us from the extreme consequences.

The greatest motive of all for taking care of our environment is to fulfill the commandments that fulfill the whole law of God—to love God and love one another. If we love God, we will care for the remarkable and wonderful gift that

He has given us in this earth. If we love one another, especially our own children, we will want to pass the earth on to them in the best shape possible, as well as passing on the appreciation of it.

God did give dominion over the earth to man, commanding man to subdue it. For most of man's history, he has seen the earth as hostile, and something that had to be constantly battled just to survive. However, for the most part man has now subdued the earth and has dominion over it. We should realize that it is not our enemy, but a gift, and one that will serve us well if we serve it well as the benevolent masters that all who are made in the image of God should be, as He is the most benevolent Master of all. As we are promised by the prophets, the earth will be restored to the paradise it was originally intended to be so that even the lion will lie down with the lamb, and children will be able to play with cobras, and no one will hurt anyone else. Obviously, we are not there yet and will not be until "the last Adam," Christ, returns to take His dominion over the earth. Even so, because man was given dominion over the earth, man will have to take the initiative to bring peace to the creation, loving it and living in harmony with it. Now is a good time to start.

However, for the most part man has now subdued the earth and has dominion over it.

I am sure some of you will quickly disagree with part of this article's perspective, especially on some of these Christian movements and their doctrines, which are sometimes presented from a liberal, political perspective. However, it is important that we understand that perspective, and why it is so prevalent. Also, as in the case of the discussion of the impact of Pat Robertson and the Christian Coalition, Pat Robertson has come out as an advocate for global warming, and is now seen as a potential ally by many liberals, which has helped to change their perspective of conservatives at least to a degree. This indicates just how powerful this issue is and could actually be one that starts to heal some of the great divisions, building at least small bridges of trust. This should be the case because these issues should not be the domain of any political party, though it certainly is not the case at this time. To share a personal perspective on some of these issues, I will occasionally make notes after a section, which will be in italics. RJ

An Independent Research Project

While discussing the impending 2004 election, my father, an ardent evangelical Christian, asserted that the evangelical community would determine the outcome of the presidential race. At the time, I naively brushed off his comment, ascribing it to his, in my opinion, somewhat extreme religious and political perspective. Upon reflection, however, it seems that his assertion may not have been that far off. It is estimated that evangelical Christians comprise 30 to 35 percent of the national population (Eskridge), and consequentially they constituted approximately one-fourth or more of voters in the last presidential election (NAE). Far from being an irrelevant group of mere laymen (as often perceived), evangelicals are a dynamic and influential community. They promote ideologies and organizations which, in turn, permeate countless aspects of American corporate, cultural, and political life. Thus for joy or chagrin, evangelical Christians have emerged as an incredibly powerful political force in the United States today (Eskridge).

It is estimated that evangelical Christians comprise 30 to 35 percent of the national population.

In his 1967 memo, Lynn White, Jr. noted that *"Human ecology is deeply conditioned by beliefs about our nature and destiny . . . that is, by religion."* He went on to advise that *"since the roots of our trouble are so largely religious, the remedy must also essentially be religious."* Because religious beliefs are so influential in shaping cultural values, many environmentalists have expressed the necessity of articulating a mainstream religious paradigm which encourages an environmental ethic. In the modern political climate, the evangelical Christian community is often viewed to be inextricably married to the Republican Party (Eskridge), and its fervent position of emphasizing economic matters at the expense of a healthy environment. Therefore, evangelical Christianity has historically been completely discarded by environmentalists in their search for a viable, ecologically sympathetic, religious perspective. However, as the environmental crisis intensifies, there is a growing necessity to win over this influential religious community to the environmental cause. Answering this call, a group of renegade evangelical leaders has emerged to instruct an evangelical environmental ethic. In a passionate attempt to shift the ecological ethic of this community, such individuals have sparked a small but growing environmental movement within the evangelical church. In doing so, these charismatic teachers derive their environmental values from a thus far unconventional and untapped source—the Bible.

This paper seeks to describe these varying discourses within the evangelical community in order to better grasp how this powerful sect of American society could potentially lend its helping hand to the current environmental crisis. While drawing from a variety of references on the subject matter, the two primary sources for this essay are evangelical Christians, Pastor Tri Robinson, Dr. Matthew Sleeth, and environmental scientist and writer Cal Dewitt. Pastor Tri Robinson leads a "green" mega-church in Boise, Idaho and has also authored the book titled, *Saving God's Green Earth.* Dr. Matthew Sleeth is a prominent ER doctor who forfeited his career to start a non-profit organization that educates evangelical Christians on environmental issues (as well as environmentalists on evangelical Christianity). He also wrote the book, *Serve God, Save the Planet: A Christian Call to Action.* Cal Dewitt is a prominent evangelical environmental scientist who founded the Au Sable Institute of Environmental Studies, a Christian university dedicated to educating the Christian community on environmental issues. He has published numerous books and essays on the subject of caring for creation.

Such individuals have sparked a small but growing environmental movement within the evangelical church.

History and Context

The evangelical movement in the United States was birthed during the Protestant revival periods of the eighteenth and early nineteenth centuries wherein it rapidly gained followers (Eskridge). While throughout history its prominence has fluctuated mildly, evangelical

Christians remain a powerful facet of American society. The term "evangelicalism" refers to a religious perspective which studies and accepts the Bible as literal truth (as opposed to metaphorical), and asserts that it is the infallible and authoritative Word of God. Furthermore, they believe that the Bible should be taken into serious account in instructing beliefs, values, and practices (DeWitt 2). The idiom "evangelical" stems from the Greek word "evangelion," which translates into English as "the good news" or "gospel" (Eskridge). This good news is generally presented as the belief in the sacrificial love of the divine Son of God, Jesus Christ, who forfeited His life for the salvation and reconciliation of the world (Dewitt 2). Moreover, evangelical Christians take an activist approach to spreading this good news in their endeavor to convert non-believers (DeWitt 2). Upon conversion to evangelical Christianity, there is a strong emphasis on a personal relationship with Jesus Christ which, in turn, further guides one's beliefs and behavior.

The evangelical community has emerged in the political realm as a conservative powerhouse known as the Religious Right.

According to the Institute for the Study of American Evangelicals, evangelical Christians entered the modern political arena during the 1970s when self-professed evangelical Christian, Jimmy Carter was elected President. Since that era, the evangelical community has emerged in the political realm as a conservative powerhouse known as the Religious Right, which has consistently supported Republican candidates and political endeavors (Eskridge). This relationship has greatly alienated evangelicals from environmental issues which have remained primarily on the platform of the Democratic Party. While reasons for the liaison of evangelicals and the Republican Party (and subsequent division from environmental concerns) abound, the primary causes stem from the modern polarization of social issues in the political sphere, an apocalyptic evangelical doctrine known as Dispensational Premillennialism, and the widespread cultural effect of the early American Manifest Destiny ideology.

Manifest Destiny

Addressing the historical alienation of evangelical Christianity from environmentalism, the Environmental Taskforce at Pastor Tri Robinson's Vineyard Christian Fellowship penned an essay titled "Why We Resist" *(Let's Tend the Garden)*. In this essay, the committee attributes one reason the evangelical church has been hesitant to embrace environmental stewardship to the cultural myth of Manifest Destiny that pervaded Christian doctrine during the founding years of the United States *(Let's Tend the Garden)*. The cultural narrative of Manifest Destiny posited that the vast American continent was providentially bequeathed to the American people by God for the specific purposes of conquering territory, expanding Western civilization, and exploiting natural resources (Hendricks).

When the Puritan settlers landed in New England, they appropriated a "New Canaan" metaphor that conjectured the settlers as the Israelites being delivered from the wilderness into an abundant land of milk and honey (Glass). One result of this cultural narrative was that the American settlers felt they had a religious license to conquer, transform, and exploit the new continent's abundant natural resources and native populations as they pleased. During the founding years of the United States, natural resources appeared bountiful and inexhaustible. However, many theorists believe that this cultural and religious approach has contributed to an American mentality which has led to excessive resource exploitation and modern environmental degradation (Glass and Hendricks).

Dominion Theology

The Manifest Destiny narrative has had vast implications on contemporary evangelical ideology. In the United States (especially amongst Christians), this ideology advanced the already present Western tradition of viewing nature as separate from humanity and as an entity which needs to be subdued and dominated for modern civilization to function (Lodrick). Furthermore, it facilitated the emergence of a Dominion Theology amongst evangelicals and other Christians (Hendricks). Dominion Theology is derived from Genesis 1:26 where it states:

Then God said, "Let us make man in our image, in our likeness and let them rule over the fish of the sea and the birds of the air, over the livestock, over all the earth and over all the creatures that move along the ground."

Adherents to Dominion Theology interpret this verse to mean that God has granted humanity authority over nature for the explicit purpose of mankind's utilization (Hendricks). This outlook devalues nature by situating the creation as a mere backdrop to humankind's spiritual relationship with a transcendent God (Langmead). Thus, evangelical social concerns tend to be anthropocentric, consequently encouraging an apathetic attitude toward other aspects of creation (Schultz). Therefore, this religious perspective has provided a religious justification for the exploitation of the environment for the economic benefit of humanity.

This religious perspective has provided a religious justification for the exploitation of the environment for the economic benefit of humanity.

The Wise Use movement has been known to successfully manipulate Dominion Theology to gain Christian supporters for its anti-environmental ideology and political activism (Hendricks). Citing one example of this dangerous relationship, environmental lawyer and author, Robert Kennedy, Jr. asserts that:

> *When the Wise Use allies hooked up with Pat Robertson's Christian Coalition, they hit a home run. Robertson's special contribution to right-wing theology was to substitute environmentalists for communists as the new threat to democracy and Christianity . . . They invoke Christianity to justify the rape of the land, violating manifold Christian precepts that requires us to be careful stewards. Rather than elevating the spirit, their interpretation of Scripture emphasizes the grimmest vision of the human condition. They embrace intolerance, selfishness, pride, and arrogance toward creation, and irresponsibility to the community and future generations (Kennedy and Hendricks).*

Pat Robertson is the founder of the Christian Coalition of America, a powerful evangelical lobbying organization, as well as creator and public figure for the prominent Christian Broadcasting Network. On Robertson's Christian Coalition of America website, it states that:

> *Increasingly a number of conservative evangelicals are succumbing to left-wing political and ideological advocacy arguments as they relate to discussion over religion and environment—arguments which have no sound scientific, economic or theological foundations (Combs).*

This article goes on to endorse drilling in the Alaskan National Wildlife Refuge (deeming it a "forsaken piece of property with huge oil reserves") and condemns congressional efforts to cut back national energy use to alleviate the negative effects of global warming (Combs), thus confirming only some of the Christian Coalition's many anti-environmental positions. Prominent evangelical leader Pat Robertson's anti-environmental advocacy is but one illustration of Dominion Theology's pervasive influence over the evangelical community.

Pat Robertson has publicly stated that he believes that global warming is a real issue.

Since this was written, Pat Robertson has publicly stated that he believes that global warming is a real issue, and his leadership in this has caused many other evangelicals to at least consider this issue more openly. In defense of Pat's position stated above about the dominance of "left-wing ideological" arguments in the environmental movements, there is a basis for this belief among many conservatives that the environmental movements have been hijacked and turned into left-wing political movements. Extreme environmental movements have made many extreme, inaccurate, and polarizing statements about conservatives and business that could not help but to provoke reaction and distrust of the environmental movements by conservatives and the business community. Pat's recent statement encouraged the consideration of the global warming issue which has been applauded as remarkable and courageous.

There are extremes on every side of almost every issue. Even if the entire environmental movement has been hijacked by liberal politicians, this does not make the issues themselves wrong. An eagle does need both a left and right wing if it is going to fly. I also use the word "hijacked" here because the environmental movement was made a political issue by a Republican President, Teddy Roosevelt, and one of the greatest environmental Presidents was another Republican, Richard Nixon. Conservation was originally a conservative issue and will be again. Hopefully, it will also remain a liberal issue, and a place where both agree and can work out the best solutions for all concerned. RJ

Dispensational Premillennialism

Dominion Theology becomes considerably more environmentally destructive when combined with an evangelical doctrine known as Dispensational Premillennialism. Dispensational Premillennialism is an eschatological worldview which asserts that in the millennia, worldwide conditions will continually worsen until the second coming of Christ when the whole of the earth will be renewed (Hodges). Due to their apocalyptic worldview, many Dispensational Premillennialists refrain from working toward any sort of enduring goal with the exception of evangelism (Hodges). Professor Dewey H. Hodges, author of an extensive essay on the subject, describes their attitude towards worldly troubles as "Why polish the brass on a sinking ship?" Thus many Dispensational Premillennialists ascribe environmental degradation, natural disasters, war, terrorism, genocide, famine, and other wide scale tragedies to signs of the fulfillment of biblical prophecy (Hodges). Due to their fervent belief in an imminent apocalypse, many Dispensational Premillennialists perceive it as unnecessary to work towards the reformation of these issues in the long run (Hodges). Hence, at best Dispensational Premillennialists perceive environmental efforts as a fruitless endeavor and at worst they welcome environmental degradation as a sign of the ever more impending second coming of Christ (Langmead).

Conservation was originally a conservative issue and will be again.

One blatant illustration of why this perspective is incompatible with an environmental ethic is found on a bumper sticker distributed by the evangelical Treasure Valley Baptist Church of Boise, Idaho, which begs the question: *Forget "Save the Earth"; What about your soul? The earth is going to burn; What about you?* (Zaleha) Unfortunately, because Dispensational Premillennialism's emphasis is eschatological (Hodges), many other environmentally significant biblical perspectives and messages (such as Jesus' messages of love and egalitarianism as well as the numerous biblical passages on stewardship, etc.) are often overlooked at its expense (Orr 1).

Dispensational Premillennialism swept through the evangelical community during the 1980s and early 1990s during which time an abundant amount of books and teachings were published on the subject (Hendricks). Moreover, it continues to have an immeasurable impact on contemporary American ideology wherein polls conducted as recently as 2004 indicate that 55 to 59 percent of Americans take the eschatological prophecies of the Bible literally (Hendricks). Such statistics suggest a wide scale lack of incentive to be concerned about the environment amongst the American evangelical community (Hendricks). Furthermore, Dispensational Premillennialism has seeped into the political realm through political figures such as President Reagan's Secretary of the Interior, James Watt, who became infamous for his claim that environmental regulation is an extraneous endeavor because the Lord will be returning soon (Hodges).

Evangelical Christians have an exceptional amount of influence in the current government.

By virtue of sheer population numbers, as well as through holding prominent political positions, evangelical Christians have an exceptional amount of influence in the current government (Orr 1). Consequently, in a controversial editorial in the journal, "Conservation Biology," Professor David Orr goes so far as to argue that the convergence of evangelical end-time theology with the conservative economic agenda is what has produced the detrimental lack of governmental progression on the increasingly vital matter of environmental regulation (Orr 1). Thus, through both its ideological and political influence the dogma of

Dispensational Premillennialism has had an immense and adverse effect on the development of a modern evangelical environmental ethic *(Let's Tend the Garden)*. In recent years, however, a growing number of evangelicals have rejected the "it's all going to burn anyway" attitude in favor of an evangelical perspective that values stewardship of creation *(Let's Tend the Garden)*.

Polarization of Social Issues in the Political Sphere

Perhaps the greatest inhibitor in the attempt to foster a modern evangelical environmental ethic has been the vast polarization of social issues within the political sphere. Many evangelicals associate environmentalism with alternative social and political issues championed by liberals. Evangelicals tend to disagree with the left-leaning social agenda which often incorporates such issues as the woman's right to abortion and gay rights (Ohlmen). Former Professor and Christian environmentalist and author, Dean Ohlmen, addresses this circumstance by stating blatantly that:

Evangelicals tend to disagree with the left-leaning social agenda which often incorporates such issues as the woman's right to abortion and gay rights.

> *Most evangelicals are political and social conservatives, and we have been brainwashed by that community to conclude that environmental protection measures are almost always misguided "liberal" policies based on "junk science...." Furthermore, Evangelicals tend to lump protection of the environment together with the lack of protection for children in the womb; we often have the irrational idea that abortion-rights advocacy and the efforts to rescue stranded animals or preserve endangered non-human species are parallel and equal hallmarks of "liberal" thought. Most fail to see how illogical it is to save the babies and then care less about the health and integrity of the environment upon which their survival depends.*

Because of such political associations, evangelicals have historically tended to discount the matter of environmental protection. Likewise, many environmentalists perceive evangelicals as inevitable sympathizers with the conservative Religious Right, a group which is renowned for its close relationship to the Republican Party, conservative economic stance

(Eskridge), and cynicism in regard to environmental concerns (Ohlmen). Therefore, environmentalists have traditionally tossed evangelical Christianity aside in its effort to affect a mainstream environmental paradigm. Many evangelical environmentalists assert that the early disjuncture of evangelicals and environmentalists stems from the hippie era of the sixties and seventies during which the environmental movement was conceptually linked to "heavy drug use, immorality and 'free love'" *(Let's Tend the Garden)*. Other theorists argue that the schism is a direct result of deliberate strategic influence perpetuated by the religious and political Right (Orr 1). Regardless of its source, however, it is evident that the division of social agendas in the political sphere has prompted many evangelicals to disregard environmental efforts altogether.

The division of social agendas in the political sphere has prompted many evangelicals to disregard environmental efforts altogether.

The aforementioned ideological factors have played an enormous role in hindering the cultivation of a modern evangelical environmental ethic. However, in recent years, as environmental concerns continue to escalate, there has emerged a growing discourse within the evangelical community which fervently advocates the protection of the environment. These revolutionary environmental advocates oppose previous anti-environmental evangelical ideologies through communicating a morally compelling message founded in the biblical values of stewardship, love, and the Christian God's personal relationship with nature. Moreover, they rearticulate environmental degradation as a moral concern that is dictated by a clear biblical mandate rather than a controversial political issue (Robinson 1). Thus, evangelical environmentalists offer a reading of the Bible which positively contributes to the nurturing of a mainstream environmental ethic.

The Stewardship Principle

One leading environmental discourse within the evangelical community is that of the principle of biblical stewardship. Stewardship is founded on the biblical mandate that humanity must maintain the garden (earth) in which God placed him (Dewitt 1). This directive, which interestingly is the first commandment given by God (Sleeth 3), is found in Genesis 2:15 where it states: **"The Lord God took the man and put him in the Garden of Eden to work it and take care of it."** Furthermore, evangelical environmentalist Calvin Dewitt notes that the Bible does not even reference the service of the earth to mankind, but conversely emphasizes the responsibility of humans to cultivate and serve the earth (Dewitt 1).

> **Stewardship is founded on the biblical mandate that humanity must maintain the garden (earth) in which God placed him.**

Stewardship is founded on a reciprocal approach wherein earth-keeping is proffered as a demonstration of gratitude for God's creation and its sustenance of mankind (Robinson 1 and Dewitt 1). In a phone interview with Pastor Tri Robinson, he provided an allegory which he uses to illustrate the principle of stewardship. He tells the story of a friend who gave him a horse (as Pastor Robinson is a rancher). He was astounded by the gift and wanted to show his friend how thankful he was for such an undeserved blessing. Thus, he determined that the best method in which he could show his friend gratitude would be through deeply valuing and caring for the horse. Pastor Robinson highlights that if his friend had come to visit and the horse had been neglected and/or mistreated, his friend would probably have interpreted this behavior as disrespect and ingratitude. Moreover, his friend would likely be very angry, disappointed, and hurt with Pastor Robinson for being so irresponsible with his precious gift. Likewise, God has provided humanity with the earth and all of its magnificent and delicate systems which are designed to serve and sustain human existence. The provision of such an invaluable gift inherently implies that mankind is expected to be concerned and to work for creation's well-being and renewal. Furthermore, God specifically commands that humans keep the earth. Therefore, by degrading the environment and mistreating the earth, Christians not only exhibit disrespect and ingratitude towards God, but they also expressly disobey His first commandment.

In his book, *Serve God, Save the Planet,* Dr. Matthew Sleeth provides another perspective on the stewardship principle. This perspective holds that the earth is on loan from God to each human generation and therefore it is every generation's responsibility to preserve it for the ultimate return of its Master. Sleeth supports this principle from the Bible verse Psalm 24:1, which affirms that **"The earth is the Lord's, and everything in it,"** and Leviticus 25:23-24 which states:

"...The land is mine and you are but aliens and my tenants.

"Throughout the country that you hold as a possession, you must provide for the redemption of the land."

Additionally, Sleeth reiterates to his readers that some day the Lord will return to reclaim His possession and, according to the Gospel of Mark, no one knows the hour or day when this will take place. In his phone interview, Robinson also addresses this circumstance through highlighting a conversation between Jesus and His disciples in the Gospel of Matthew. During the discussion, the disciples inquire about the end times and Jesus' second coming. Jesus answers them with the following warning:

This perspective holds that the earth is on loan from God to each human generation.

"...Watch out that no one deceives you.

"For many will come in my name, claiming,

'I am the Christ,' and will deceive many. You will hear of wars and rumors of wars, but see to it that you are not alarmed. Such things must happen, but the end is still to come.

"No one knows about that day or hour, not even the angels in heaven, nor the Son, but only the Father.

"Therefore keep watch, because you do not know on what day your Lord will come.

"But understand this: If the owner of the house had known at what time of night the thief was coming, he would have kept watch and would not have let his house be broken into.

"So you also must be ready, because the Son of Man will come at an hour when you do not expect him.

"Who then is the faithful and wise servant, whom the master has put in charge of the servants in his household to give them their food at the proper time?

"It will be good for that servant whose master finds him doing so when he returns" (Matthew 24:4-6, 36, 42-46).

Teachings and sermons on the Parable of the Talents are popular in evangelical circles.

Therefore, both Sleeth and Robinson assert that it is pertinent for Christians to constantly prepare for Jesus' return by being faithful stewards of the environment. The stewardship perspective opposes the anti-environmental sentiments of Dispensational Premillennialism through positing that, because Christians do not know when the Lord will return, it is therefore necessary to continually conduct oneself in a faithful and obedient manner. Both authors contend that, naturally, such behavior would encompass the biblical charge to cultivate and keep the earth. Accordingly, disavowing efforts to protect the environment due to the assumption of an imminent apocalypse is in direct defiance of Christ's counsel to be faithful stewards.

The stewardship principle is arguably the most popular and well-received environmental ethics narrative amongst evangelicals. One reason this discourse resonates favorably with evangelicals is because a discourse of biblical stewardship is already a prevalent theme within the Christian community (Bakken). Teachings and sermons on the Parable of the Talents (wherein a man entrusts his servants with his property and the servants who are faithful and resourceful are rewarded) are popular in evangelical circles. However, the most common application of the stewardship principle has thus far been fiscally-oriented. Furthermore, the stewardship principle maintains a largely anthropogenic perspective towards the environment wherein nature is most often objectified as an entity which needs to be mediated through God-human interactions (Bakken). This position does not complicate previous evangelical anthropogenic views which emphasize the God-human spiritual relationship. Thus the concept of environmental stewardship permits evangelicals to easily identify with and understand its tenets and therefore they are more likely to accept its conclusions as valid.

Ecocentric critics argue that this perspective is problematic because it reinforces the conceptual separation of humanity from creation as well as furthers the hierarchal relationship of mankind above nature. They assert that, consequently, the stewardship narrative has the potential to diminish creation as valuable in its own right (Bakken). Further obscuring the discourse of environmental stewardship are organizations and individuals who use stewardship jargon as a euphemism for Dominion Theology and other environmentally exploitative ideologies (Bakken). However, despite such opposition many Christian environmentalists continue to embrace the stewardship principle as an adaptable and useful interpretation of biblical environmental ethics (Bakken).

The Bible clearly indicates that God has a loving relationship with all of His creation.

Regardless of its possible disparities, many critics grant that the environmental stewardship narrative is a vast improvement over Dominion Theology and other anti-environmental evangelical ideologies and therefore is a valuable hortatory discourse in this precarious era of environmental crisis (Bakken).

God's Love for Creation

Another prominent discourse within the evangelical environmental community highlights that the Bible clearly indicates that God has a loving relationship with all of His creation. Many evangelical environmentalists observe that when God created **"the great creatures of the sea and every living and moving thing with which the water teems,**

according to their kinds, and every winged bird according to its kind" (see Genesis 1:21), He saw that His creation was good. God then proceeds to bless His creation by commanding, **"Be fruitful and multiply, and fill the waters in the seas, and let birds multiply on the earth" (see Genesis 1:22 NAS).** Addressing God's concern for creation, prominent evangelical environmental scientist, Calvin Dewitt, affirms what he titles the Fruitfulness Principle. The Fruitfulness Principle asserts that *"people may enjoy the fruit of God's creation but must not destroy its fruitfulness"* (Dewitt 1). It is founded on Ezekiel 34:18-20 which states,

> **Is it too little for you to have eaten up the good pasture, that you must tread down with your feet the residue of your pasture—and to have drunk of the clear waters, that you must foul the residue with your feet?**
>
> **And as for My flock, they eat what you have trampled with your feet, and they drink what you have fouled with your feet.**
>
> **Therefore thus says the Lord GOD to them: "Behold, I Myself will judge between the fat and the lean sheep" (NKJV).**

A plethora of nature imagery is woven throughout the Bible.

In his essay, "A Contemporary Evangelical Perspective," Dewitt employs this principle while addressing the problem of species extinction. He contends that *"preserving Creation's fruitfulness preserves biotic species whose interactions with each other, and with land and water, form the fabric of the biosphere. Our fruitfulness should not be at the expense of the fruitfulness of other creatures"* (Dewitt 1).

Further signifying God's affection for nature, the Bible magnificently declares God's providential care and concern for trees, cows, streams, goats, donkeys, and lions (see Psalm 104). Moreover, a plethora of nature imagery is woven throughout the Bible (Sleeth 3). For example, Dr. Matthew Sleeth notes that in the Bible the tree is often used as a symbol of God (particularly in verses that discuss the Garden of Eden and in Revelation 22:2), and that interestingly there are over five hundred references to trees throughout the Bible (Sleeth 1). Sleeth emphasizes that while the Bible does infer that God has a special relationship with mankind, He also groans when a single sparrow falls from the sky (Sleeth 1). God's love for all of His creation is evidenced by the fact that when God flooded the earth He commanded Noah to build an ark in order to preserve both humankind and **"every creeping thing of the earth" (see Genesis 6:20 NKJV).** Furthermore, following the flood God made a covenant (never to flood the earth again) not only with mankind but with **"every living creature . . . that is on the earth" (see Genesis 9:15-17 NKJV).**

Perhaps the most telling display of God's love for all of creation is found in the Gospel of John which declares: **"For God so loved the world that He gave His only begotten Son" (see John 3:16 NKJV).** Therefore, God's love for the world is so great that He sacrificed His only Son, not for humans alone, but for the salvation of all of His beloved creation. This commonly quoted verse reveals a telling display of the high value and affection which God Himself placed on His creation—the world and all it contains, together—man, beast, and nature.

God's love for the world is so great that He sacrificed His only Son, not for humans alone, but for the salvation of all of His beloved creation.

Evangelical environmentalists argue that based on the aforementioned references, it is clear that God exceedingly loves and cares about the entirety of creation. Therefore, human degradation of the environment is a blatant affront to its Creator. Cal Dewitt addresses this scenario by providing a metaphor which contends that *"honoring the Master Artist while trampling the Master Artist's works is an intolerable hypocrisy that must be corrected"* (Dewitt 1). Dewitt openly admonishes dualistic interpretations of Christianity that serve to devalue the natural world through overemphasizing the God-human spiritual connection. He acknowledges that while the Bible does indicate that God has a unique affinity for humankind, it also undoubtedly communicates God's profound love and regard for the rest of nature. Dewitt continues to note that nature elicits the *"praise, pride, and protection of the Creator, irrespective of a utilitarian purpose*" (Dewitt 1), and thus has intrinsic value simply because it is the work of the Creator (Dewitt 1). Therefore, if evangelicals are to read the Bible as a literal text it is of the utmost importance that they take into account not only God's relationship with humanity, but also God's love for the rest of creation.

This narrative is an authoritative tool for evangelical environmentalists who seek to reconceptualize evangelicals' relationship to nature. It is principally based on biblical text and therefore carries a unique power in positively affecting an evangelical environmental ethic. The Bible commands Christians to **"love the LORD your God, to walk in his ways, and to keep his commands, decrees and laws" (see Deuteronomy 30:16).** Therefore, Christians must observe God's love for creation and abide by the ways in which He formed the harmonic laws and processes of the natural world. Because evangelicals interpret the Bible in a literal manner, and place an extraordinary emphasis on a loving, respectful, and interactive relationship with God, this narrative presents a persuasive incentive for them to realign their perceptions of nature with God's perception of nature. Through this lens, nature is rearticulated as a sacred and precious work of God, the Creator. Therefore, to serve God in the utmost manner requires evangelicals to reassess environmental degradation as an affront to the Creator.

To serve God in the utmost manner requires evangelicals to reassess environmental degradation as an affront to the Creator.

THE TWO BOOK FAITH

Another significant and powerful discourse emerging in the evangelical community is the articulation of a Two Book Faith. This perspective asserts that a holistic interpretation of Christianity must be based on the interactive study of both works of God—the Holy Bible and His creation (Robinson 2). Furthermore, it affirms that God, being the Author and Creator of the universe, reveals His character through His creation (Dewitt 2). Cal Dewitt has spearheaded efforts to convey the message of a Two Book Faith and its subsequent implications for environmental protection. He has written many eloquent and persuasive essays and books on the subject and is cited by numerous evangelical environmentalists (including Pastor Robinson). In his youth, Dewitt discovered the second article of the Belgic Confession of the Christian Reformed Church (circa the 16th century) which is as follows:

> *Article II: By What Means God Is Made Known to Us*
> *We know him by two means:*
> *First, by the creation, preservation, and government of the universe;*
> *which is before our eyes*
> *as a most elegant book*
> *wherein all creatures,*
> *great and small,*
> *are as so many characters*
> *leading us to see clearly*
> *the invisible things of God*
> *even his everlasting power*
> *and divinity*
> *as the Apostle Paul says (Romans 1:20).*
> *All these things are sufficient to convince men*
> *and leave them without excuse.*
> *Second, he makes himself known to us more openly by his holy and divine Word, as much as we need in this life, for his glory and for the salvation of his own (Dewitt 2).*

All creatures, great and small, are as so many characters leading us to see clearly the invisible things of God.

This ancient declaration serves as an eloquent and important foundation for Dewitt's modern articulation of the Two Book Faith.

Among other verses, the Two Book Faith perspective is based on Romans 1:20 where the Apostle Paul writes,

> **For since the creation of the world God's invisible qualities—his eternal power and divine nature—have been clearly seen, being understood from what is made, so that men are without excuse.**

Psalm 19:1-4 pronounces:

> **The heavens declare the glory of God; the skies proclaim the work of his hands.**
>
> **Day after day they pour forth speech; night after night they display knowledge.**
>
> **There is no speech or language where their voice is not heard.**
>
> **Their voice goes out into all the earth, their words to the ends of the world.**

Thus, the natural world and all of its complex and interconnected systems, living and non-living beings, demonstrate the character and testimony of God. Catholic eco-theologian Thomas Berry affirmed this perspective, when he noted that *"the universe itself is for us 'the primary mode of God's presence"* (quoted in Gottlieb). Therefore, as a principal medium through which humans experience the nature of God, the natural world holds inestimable inherent value.

It is imperative that evangelicals study and abide by the laws of nature as well as the commandments of the Bible.

The Two Book Faith dialogue does not merely paint creation as a valuable projection of God's character. It emphasizes that, furthermore, nature is a crucial tool which God provided in order to instruct Christians on how to correctly live in this world. Therefore, in seeking to live a truly godly lifestyle, it is imperative that evangelicals study and abide by the laws of nature as well as the commandments of the Bible. Consequently, human degradation of the environment reflects a clear departure from the decree of God. Reiterating this vital point, Dewitt quotes the sobering utterance of the Prophet Hosea:

> **There is no faithfulness, no love, no acknowledgment of God in the land.**
>
> **There is only cursing, lying and murder, stealing and adultery; they break all bounds, and bloodshed follows bloodshed.**

Because of this the land mourns, and all who live in it waste away;

the beasts of the field and the birds of the air and the fish of the sea are dying (see Hosea 4:1-3).

Dewitt goes on to reason that the current environmental crisis poses an ethical concern which mirrors Christians' thus far erroneous attitudes toward the natural world and creation's instruction on sustainable living (Dewitt 2). Thus, in approaching an ethical solution to environmental destruction, Dewitt asserts that the appropriate response must be *"one that addresses what we consider to be of ultimate importance in our lives and how we think we ought to live, one that reflects morally on how we understand and relate to nature"* (Dewitt 2). Dewitt proceeds to declare that if evangelicals do indeed believe God to be *"the creator, owner and sustainer"* of the natural world, then human induced degradation of His creation must be viewed as a spiritual crisis. He argues that this response is essential precisely because one's manner of relating to God's creation reflects how one understands and relates to God (Dewitt 2). The discourse of a Two Book Faith reframes nature as a sacred teacher which powerfully communicates the character of God to humanity and furthermore gives His instructions on how to correctly live in this world. Accordingly, efforts to protect the environment are successfully rearticulated as a holy and necessary endeavor.

Efforts to protect the environment are successfully rearticulated as a holy and necessary endeavor.

Jon Amos Comenius is regarded as one of the men to most impact the modern world. As "the father of modern education," his vision that all children should receive an education, not just the children of the nobility, was rooted in his vision that a generation would arise to fulfill the Great Commission by preaching the gospel to every nation. It was also Comenius who first stated that "nature is God's second book," as he taught and promoted a deep love for creation that was based in a deep love for his Creator. Comenius therefore advocated studying and loving the creation in order to better understand and love the

Creator, as the creation was an obvious reflection of the Creator. This led to Comenius becoming the first to use illustrations in books and to coin the phrase "A picture is worth a thousand words." Few have helped to illuminate the world like Jon Amos Comenius, whose teachings in many areas remain even ahead of our time, though written nearly four hundred years ago. In them there is a remarkable link and unity between "God's first book," the Bible, and "God's second book," nature. RJ

Love and Action

God's love and regard for nature alone dictates that, in loving and serving God, evangelical Christians have a moral responsibility to protect His creation from destructive exploitation. However, many evangelical environmentalists emphasize that environmental deterioration also significantly reduces the well-being of humankind. Therefore, in abiding by Jesus' command to **"love the LORD your God with all your heart, with all your soul, with all your strength, and with all your mind, and your neighbor as yourself" (Luke 10:27 NKJV),** evangelicals must work to alleviate ecological degradation that causes undue harm to humans, as well as the environment.

Evangelical Christians have a moral responsibility to protect His creation from destructive exploitation.

Dr. Matthew Sleeth notes that for him, the most significant biblical passage is Jesus' Parable of the Good Samaritan. This parable tells the story of a Jewish man who was robbed, beaten, and left for dead by the side of the road. A priest and a Levite (notably people from similar backgrounds to that of the Jewish man) pass him by and do nothing; one man even feels sympathetic but does not act on his feelings. However, a Samaritan (a fact that indicates he was from a community that was ostracized by Jewish society) sees the injured man and takes pity on him by mending his wounds and carrying him to an inn where he can recover. He even pays for the injured man's full room and board while he recuperates. Most interpretations of this parable recognize that Jesus uses this allegory to demonstrate Christians' responsibility to care for our neighbors no matter how foreign they are to us (Sleeth 3). Therefore, evangelical environmentalists contend that Jesus' message of compassion necessitates that Christians take up environmental concerns which cause undue harm to our neighbors (Robinson 1).

Sleeth goes on to assert that this responsibility naturally encompasses not only people who are currently affected by environmental degradation, but future generations as well (Sleeth 1). Moreover, in the Gospel of Matthew, Jesus explicitly states, **"Assuredly, I say to you, inasmuch as you did it to one of the least of these My brethren, you did it to Me" (Matthew 25:40 NKJV).** Jesus instructs Christians to care for the **"least"** among society as they would behave towards Jesus Himself. Based on this biblical ethic, numerous evangelical environmentalists contend that ecologically destructive practices which adversely and inequitably affect the poorest communities of the world (such as environmental degradation related to ecojustice, global warming, water contamination, etc.) are manifestly incongruent with Jesus' message to care for "**the least of these"** (Sleeth and Robinson).

> **"I had to start looking at the planet as though it were my patient too."**

Dr. Matthew Sleeth's interest in environmental issues intensified after he experienced firsthand skyrocketing increases in cancer and asthma rates among his hospital patients. He attributes the escalation of chronic diseases to the reality that because of the current Western standard of living, humans live in a sea of toxic chemicals and air pollution (Sleeth 2). After years of watching patients fall ill and die from preventable conditions, Sleeth decided it was time to try a new approach. After fervently praying to God for guidance, the answer became clear to him—as he describes his epiphany: *"I had to start looking at the planet as though it were my patient too."*

Sleeth maintains that the dominant consumer culture is the primary root of environmental degradation (he specifically references air pollution, global toxicification, and climate change as the major culprits). Thus, evangelical Christians have a moral imperative to embrace lifestyle changes which alleviate their contributions to the mounting environmental crisis. Sleeth advises evangelicals to be mindful of Jesus' famous caveat that **"faith without works is dead" (see James 2:26).** Furthermore, the Bible clearly states it is a sin to know what is right and not to do it (see James 4:17). Sleeth articulates a compelling narrative which emphasizes personal action and more specifically an anti-consumerism lifestyle. He founds this narrative on Jesus' model of sacrificial love, simple living, and action and urges Western evangelicals to consider whether their own lifestyle choices adhere to Jesus' exemplar.

It is critical to reframe the issue as a biblical and moral mandate rather than a political controversy.

Conclusion

There are a variety of ideological factors which predispose evangelical Christians to take an anti-environmental stance. However, as Pastor Tri Robinson notes, evangelical opposition to environmentalism is nearly always based on political reasoning. Additionally, a holistic reading of biblical values clearly indicates a mandate to protect and care for the environment. Demonstrating this pivotal point, Pastor Robinson maintains that he has never heard a valid biblical rebuttal to his message of creation care. Thus, in order to persuade an evangelical audience to embrace environmentalism, it is critical to reframe the issue as a biblical and moral mandate rather than a political controversy.

Evangelical environmentalists have articulated dynamic and persuasive environmental discourses which are rapidly gaining resonance within the evangelical community. These discourses encompass the biblical values of environmental stewardship, love, and compassion, and project an evangelical audience that embodies such ethics. As the environmental crisis intensifies and more and more evangelicals embrace an environmental ethic, this influential community could provide a substantial resource for environmental efforts. Furthermore, if the evangelical community does indeed take on an environmental perspective, it could have an enormous influence on the adoption of a mainstream environmental ethic. ■

Anna Jane Joyner is a recent graduate from the University of North Carolina where she studied Rhetoric and Environmental Studies. She has done extensive research on faith-based environmental discourse. Anna is currently working at the National Sierra Club in Washington, D.C. where she works to build partnerships between the environmental and faith communities. She enjoys green tea, dogs, reading, thought-provoking conversation, kayaking, yoga and Pilates, healthy cooking, good friends, traveling, and adventures. For more information on faith-based environmental initiatives, contact Anna Jane at: AJJoyner@gmail.com

We do not inherit the earth
from our ancestors,
we borrow it from our children.

—Native American Proverb

Don't blow it—
good planets are hard to find.

—Quoted in Time

Mustard Seeds of Wisdom

BIBLIOGRAPHY

Bakken, Peter W. "Stewardship." The Encyclopedia of Religion and Nature (2005):1598-1599. Nov. 2006. www.religionandnature.com/ern/S.pdf.

Boyd, Heather H. "Christianity and the Environment in the American Public." Journal for the Scientific Study of Religion 38.1 (1999): 36-44.

DeWitt, Calvin B. "A Contemporary Evangelical Perspective." The Greening of Faith: God, the Environment, and the Good Life. Eds. John E. Carroll, Paul Brockelman, and Mary Westfall. Hanover, NH: University Press of New England, 1997. 79-104.

DeWitt, Calvin B. "Christianity (7i)- An Evangelical Perspective on Faith and Nature." The Encyclopedia of Religion and Nature (2005): 369-371. Nov. 2006. www.religionandnature.com/ern/C.pdf.

Eskridge, Larry. Defining Evangelicalism. 2006. Institute for the Study of American Evangelicals at Wheaton College, Wheaton, IL. Dec. 2006, www.wheaton.edu/isae/defining_evangelicalism.html.

Glass, Matthew. "Manifest Destiny." The Encyclopedia of Religion and Nature (2005): 1038-1044. Dec 2006. www.religionandnature.com/ern/M.pdf.

Gottlieb, Roger S. *A Greener Faith: Religious Environmentalism and Our Planet's Future.* New York, New York: Oxford University Press, 2006.

Guth, James L. et al. "Faith and the Environment: Religious Beliefs and Attitudes on Environmental Policy." American Journal of Poltical Science 39.2 (1995): 364-382.

Henderson, David. "Evangelicals Are Conservationists." Conservation Biology 19.6 (2005): 1687-1688.

Hendricks, Stephenie. *Divine Destruction: Wise Use, Dominion Theory and the Making of American Environmental Policy.* Hoboken, New Jersey: Melville House Publishing, 2005.

Hermann, Claire. "An Evangelical Call to Action: A Textual Analysis of the Evangelical Climate Initiative Website." Unpublished Paper. 2006.

Hodges, Dewey H. Orthodox Views of Eschatology: Dispensational Premillennialism. 30 Dec. 2006. Georgia Institute of Technology, Atlanta, Georgia. 4 Jan. 2007. www.ae.gatech.edu/people/dhodges/papers/ESCHAT.pdf.

Holland, Laurel D., and J. Scott Carter. "Words V. Deeds: A Comparison of Religious Belief and Environmental Action." Sociological Spectrum 25 (2005): 739-1753.

Keller, Catherine. "The Heat Is On: Apocalyptic Rhetoric and Climate Change." Ecotheology 5.7 (1999): 40-58.

Kennedy Jr., Robert F. *Crimes Against Nature: How George W. Bush and His Corporate Pals Are Plundering the Country and Hijacking Our Democracy.* New York, New York: HarperCollins Publishers, 2004.

Langmead, Ross. "Ecojustice Principles: Challenges for the Evangelical Perspective." Ecotheology 5.5/6 (1998-99): 162-172.

Larsen, David K. "The Evangelical Environmental Network." The Encyclopedia of Religion and Nature (2005): 624-625. Dec. 2006. www.religionandnature.com/ern/E.pdf.

Let's Tend the Garden. 2006. The Environmental Taskforce at Vineyard Christian Fellowship, Boise, Idaho. 24 Dec. 2006. www.letstendthegarden.org.

Lodrick, Deryck O. "Domestication." The Encyclopedia of Religion and Nature (2005): 502-504. Dec 2006. www.religionandnature.com/ern/D.pdf.

Ohlmen, Dean. 21 Reasons That Evangelicals Don't "Get" Creation Care. Dec. 2005. Restoring Eden: Christians for Environmental Stewardship, La Center, WA. 8 Jan. 2007. www.restoringeden.org/resources/Ohlman/21Reasons/.

Orr, David W. "Armageddon Versus Extinction." Conservation Biology 19.2 (2005): 290-292.

Orr, David W. "A Response." Conservation Biology 19.6 (2005): 1697-1698.

Robinson, Tri. Phone Interview. 9 Nov. 2006.

Robinson, Tri. *Saving God's Green Earth.* Norcross, GA: Ampelon Publishing, 2006.

Shultz, Wesley P., Lynnette Zelezny, and Nancy J. Dalrymple. "A Multinational Perspective on the Relation Between Judeo-Christian Beliefs and Environmental Perspectives." Environment and Behavior 32 (2000): 576-591.

Sleeth, J. Matthew. Internet Interview. 8 Nov. 2006.

Sleeth, J. Matthew. Phone Interview. 21 Nov. 2006.

Sleeth, J. Matthew. *Serve God, Save the Planet: A Christian Call to Action.* White River Junction, VT: Chelsea Green Publishing, 2006.

Van Dyke, Fred. "Between Heaven and Earth—Evangelical Engagement in Conservation." Conservation Biology 19.6 (2005): 1693-1696.

Combs, Roberta. Washington Weekly Review of the Christian Coalition of America. 7 Apr. 2006. Christian Coalition of America, Washington, DC. 1 Jan. 2007. www.cc.org/content.cfm?srch=global+warming.

White Jr., Lynn. (1967). "The Historical Roots of Our Ecological Crisis." Science, 155, (1203-1207); www.zbi.ee/~kalevi/lwhite.htm.

Zaleha, Bernie. Jesus: The Mystery. 15 Sep. 2002. Fund for Christian Ecology, Boise, Idaho. 2 Jan. 2007. www.christianecology.org/Jesus.html.

NEW PRODUCTS

The Harvest

by Rick Joyner

NEW COMPACT SIZE

What is about to come upon the earth is not just a revival or another awakening; it is a veritable revolution. This vision was given in order to begin awakening those who are destined to radically change the course and even the very definition of Christianity.

—Rick Joyner

Softcover, 304 pgs. Item #RJ1-057 Retail $8.99

Our Price $7.00

You Save $1.99

You May All Prophesy

by Steve Thompson

NEW COMPACT SIZE

This has been called the best and most practical book written on the prophetic ministry and gifts by major Christian leaders. This should be required reading for all Christians.

—Rick Joyner

Softcover, 216 pgs. Item #ST1-003 Retail $8.99

Our Price $7.00

You Save $1.99

MorningStar
Teachings from MorningStar

John & Barbara
Buneck
THE
NEHEMIAH
PROJECT
The Capital Campaign to Restore H.I.M.
Nearly 200 Rooms
Have Been Sponsored
Nearly 200 H.I.M. retreat rooms have been sponsored through
The Nehemiah Project. Would you llike to join with us?
VIEW AVAILABLE ROOMS THROUGH A PANORAMIC VIEW:
WWW.HERITAGEINTERNATIONAL.ORG
JOIN THIS IMPORTANT PROJECT FOR THESE TIMES
• Call us at 1-800-542-0278
• Visit us online at www.HeritageInternational.org
• Write us at 375 Star Light Drive, Fort Mill, SC 29715

MorningStar Ministries Presents
GOOD NEWS TV
A Prophetic Perspective of World News
MorningStar has launched its newest television program, Good News TV.
The goal of Good News TV is to grow in prophetic revelation
and give a kingdom perspective on current events,
bringing you the best news the world has ever heard.
Watch Thursday at 9 P.M. EST
God Channel on Direct TV (Channel 365)
MorningStar
GOD
Also on The God Channel – The MorningStar Show
With Rick Joyner and Special Guests – Tuesday at 9 P.M. EST
For program listings outside the U.S., please visit www.God.tv.

MorningStar
Website
www.MorningStarMinistries.org
Word for the Week from Rick Joyner • Special Bulletins for
Current Events • Online Store With Books and Music • Conference
Information • Q &A With Rick Joyner • MorningStar School of
Ministry Information • MorningStar Fellowships - Charlotte •
Wilkesboro • Winston - Salem • Wilmington • MorningStar
Subscriptions - Journal • Prophetic Bulletin • Message of the
Month • Itineraries ... AND MUCH MORE

RESTORED AND ALIVE AGAIN

H.I.M. Conference Center

In the mid 1980s, Heritage USA and PTL Ministries was one of the most celebrated locations in the world. After the PTL era, Heritage sat desolate until 2004 when MorningStar purchased the Grand Hotel, Main Street, and Conference Center. Now ministries, churches, and Christians from around the world are coming back. **Consider hosting your conference or retreat at historic Heritage.**

H.I.M. Retreat Center

The newly restored property now hosts five international ministries, all within walking distance of H.I.M. Guest rooms are available for those wishing to attend any weekly service, conference, or to those who are just seeking a personal retreat. **Reserve your room today.**

For reservations and information:

- Call us at 1-800-542-0278
- Visit us online at www.HeritageInternational.org
- Write to us at 375 Star Light Drive, Fort Mill, SC 29715

Statement of Ownership, Management, and Circulation

(Required by 39 U.S.C. 3685)

1. Publication Title: The Morning Star Journal®
2. Publication No.: 0129-03
3. Filing Date: October 1, 2007
4. Issue frequency: Quarterly
5. No. of issues published annually: 4
6. Annual Subscription Price: $20.00 U.S.; $30.00 Int'l
7. Complete Mailing Address of Known Office of Publication:
   375 Star Light Drive, Fort Mill, SC 29715
   Contact person: David Hart, Telephone: 803-802-5544, ext. 230
8. Complete Mailing Address of General Office of Publisher: same as #7
9. Publisher: MorningStar Publications,
   375 Star Light Drive, Fort Mill, SC 29715
   Editor: Rick Joyner, 375 Star Light Drive, Fort Mill, SC 29715
   Managing Editor: Deborah Joyner Johnson,
   375 Star Light Drive, Fort Mill, SC 29715
10. Owner: MorningStar Fellowship Church,
    375 Star Light Drive, Fort Mill, SC 29715
11. There are no Bondholders, Mortgagees, or Other Security Holders.
12. The purpose, function, and nonprofit status of this organization and the exempt status for federal income tax purposes has not changed during the preceding 12 months.
13. Publication Title: The Morning Star Journal®
14. Issue Date of Circulation Date Below:
15. Extent and Nature of Circulation

	Average No. Copies Each Issue During Preceding 12 Months	No. Copies of Single Issue Published Nearest to Filing Date
a. Total No. of Copies (Net Press Run)	14,078	15,131
b. Paid and/or Requested Circulation		
(1)Paid/Requested Outside-County Mail Subscriptions	6,511	5,943
(2)Paid In-County Subscriptions	104	137
(3)Sales Through Dealers and Carriers, Street Vendors, and Counter Sales, and Other Non-USPS Paid Distribution	0	0
(4)Other Classes Mailed Through the USPS	1,305	480
c. Total Paid and/or Requested Circulation	7,920	6,560
d. Free Distribution by Mail		
(1) Outside-County	0	0
(2) In-County	0	0
(3) Other Classes Mailed Through the USPS	0	0
e. Free Distribution Outside the Mail	170	172
f. Total Free Distribution	170	172
g. Total Distribution	8,090	6,732
h. Copies Not Distributed	5,988	8,399
i. Total Sum of 15g. and h.)	14,078	15,131
j. Percent Paid and/or Requested Circulation	99%	99%

16. This Statement of Ownership will be printed in the Vol.17-4 issue of this publication.

David Hart, Office Business Manager, August 23, 2007